RED LIGHT WOMEN of DEATH VALLEY

ROBIN FLINCHUM

THE History PRESS

Published by The History Press
Charleston, SC 29403
www.historypress.net

First published 2015

Manufactured in the United States

ISBN 978.1.46711.751.7

Library of Congress Control Number: 2015945067

Notice: The information in this book is true and complete to the best of our knowledge. It is offered without guarantee on the part of the author or The History Press. The author and The History Press disclaim all liability in connection with the use of this book.

CONTENTS

ACKNOWLEDGEMENTS

Literally hundreds of people all over the country helped me to write this book. Trying to tell the life stories of women who moved around a lot was challenging and required the help of amateur and professional historians and genealogists, private and public archivists, clerks, coroners, librarians, activists, other writers, friends, relatives and assorted well-wishers cheering me on.

Since I have been working on this book a very long time and have lost some of my files along the way, I am bound to forget some of the people and places who contributed to this work. But ultimately every single tiny piece of information helped me to understand and flesh out the stories of these women's lives. Every little nugget uncovered by a librarian on the other side of the country, every brief notation in a dust-covered ledger book, every little mention in a historical newspaper—all these things were storytelling gold to me, and I could not have gathered them without a tremendous amount of assistance.

To my friend Judy Palmer, as always, goes a great deal of the credit, for she helped me find the path, not to mention so many of the details. Her work on the Kitty Tubb biography made the telling of that story possible. Thanks also to Mary and Carma Roper and the clerks at the Inyo County Recorder's Office; Beth Porter, Jon Klusmire and the seriously intrepid Roberta Harlan of the Eastern California Museum; Alan Metscher and Eva LaRue of the Central Nevada Museum, and especially to Alan for sharing stories and information that would no longer exist without his careful and chivalrous protection; Suzy McCoy of the Beatty Museum and Robert McCracken of the Nye County Town History Project; Susan Sorrells and Mary King of the Shoshone Museum; all the friendly clerks at the Nye County Clerk's and Recorder's Offices; Kathy Hodges of the Idaho State Historical Society and a fine private researcher; Ken Lenger of Deep Enough Press; Blair Davenport and Greg Cox of the Death Valley National Park Service archives; Guy Rocha and the Nevada State Library and Archives; Phillip Earl and the Nevada State Historical Society; Sally Zanjani, Emmett and Ruth Harder, Cliff Walker and the Mojave River Valley Museum; the Kern County Hall of Records; the Storey County Clerk's Office; the Esmeralda County Clerk's Office; the Tuolumne County Genealogical Society; the Mahoning County Clerk's Office; the Mahoning County Vital Records Office; the Mahoning County Historical Society; the University of Nevada–Las Vegas and Reno Special Collections libraries; the Bakersfield Public Library Genealogy Room; Leo Schafer, Steve Green, Joanne Goodwin, Barb Brents, Cecile and Roger Vargo of Explore Historic California, who first introduced me to Lola Travis and took me to the ruins where her rowdy saloon once stood; the late Robert Likes and Mike Patterson of Cerro Gordo; Lola Gillespie Miller and Paul Miller, who made Lola come alive and gave us the gift of seeing her face; Carrie Schikora, who shared precious and delicate family stories about Diamond Tooth Lil; Jacqui Rogers, for whom blood was thicker than pride; Vance Gilliam, David Wright, Barbara Hegne, Robert Palazzo, Jacque Sunstrand and Kari Coughlin, who laid all the groundwork for so much of the Rhyolite work that appears in this book; Shirley Harding; DeeAnn Rossetti; the now defunct but invaluable Death-Valley.us; Pam Burgess of the Ohio Genealogical Society; the San Diego Historical Society; Todd Memorial Chapel in Pomona; Serena Steiner of Calico Ghost Town; the Ballard Historical Society; Judy Tubb, Virginia Goodsen and Nancy Tubb Petersen; Kent Stoddard of the Mono County Historical Society; Terri Geisinger of Bodie; Barbara Hegne; and Ron Miller.

Special thanks to Hiya Swanhuyser for breaking down the dam so the words could flow.

And those are just the people and places whose names I either wrote down or remembered. But there were so many others who helped me find what seem like a thousand other details.

And, as always, I'm grateful for the quiet and beauty of my desert home and the love and support of my husband and son and my mother, who cheers me on.

INTRODUCTION

This book was a work in progress for a very long time. Originally, it wasn't going to be about sex workers in particular. It was going to be about all the amazing women who came to Death Valley country in the days before air conditioning, GPS and Wi-Fi and who learned to live in and love this extreme, extraordinary landscape.

I wanted to tell the stories of women who had been overlooked and forgotten. Back then, I had the idea that prostitutes, as a result of their more adventurous lives, had already been given a fair share of the limelight. But somehow, their stories continued to draw my attention. Bit by bit, fact by unexpected fact, I kept learning things about these women that amazed me, and I began to realize that only small parts of their stories had been told—that prostitutes, as they most often appeared in history, were no more than cardboard cutouts. Some sensational event brought them into the public eye, and they became frozen in that moment in time. The scene then repeated over and over in later histories. But I was discovering that if I looked below the surface of those moments, there were even more amazing stories to be found in the quiet, everyday details of these women's lives.

And while I learned these things retroactively about a group of women I had never met, I was also having a parallel experience in real time with one of the dearest women I have ever known. It was through witnessing, first as an old friend and then as a reporter, her very public arrest for prostitution that I came to have a better understanding of the material I was gathering for this book.

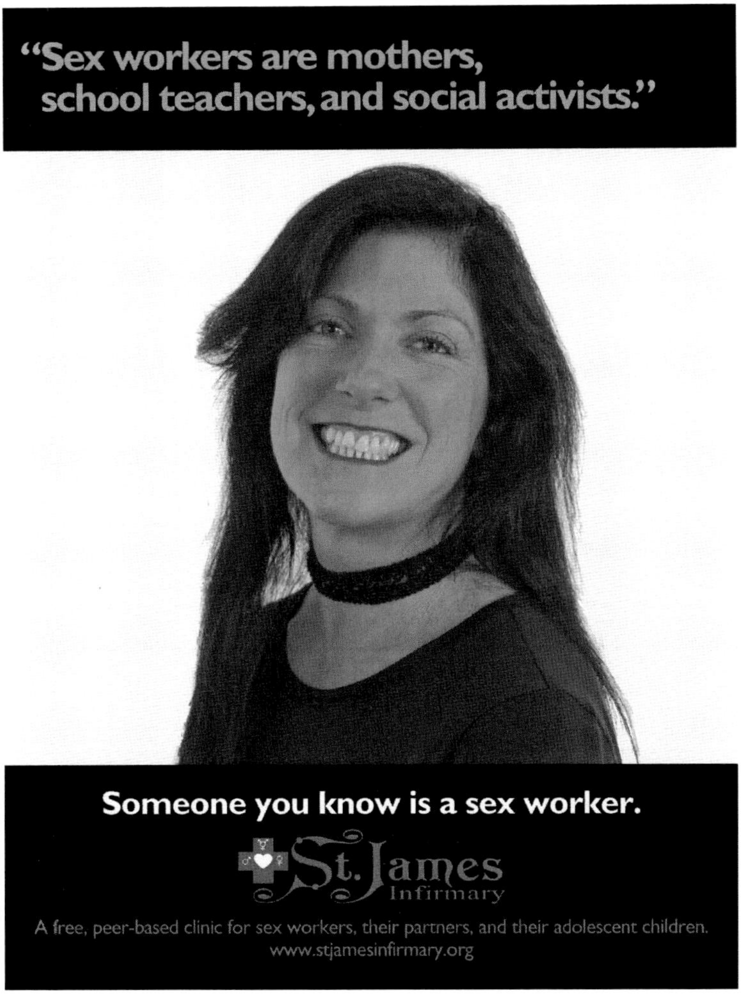

Shannon Williams (1964–2015) from the media campaign "Someone You Know Is a Sex Worker," St. James Infirmary, 2011. *Photograph by Barbara DeGenevieve and Rachel Schreiber.*

It was in the early 1990s that I first met my friend Shannon Williams. She, five feet, two inches, with an hourglass figure and wearing motorcycle boots, was being clubbed by the police at an anti-war demonstration, and I was covering the event for the college paper. I would write about her and her friends a lot that year, and I would fall in love with them all. They would become my friends, and then they would become my surrogate family.

I would, with a sense of deep responsibility and secret pride, act as Shannon's labor coach when she was pregnant with her first child. I remember leaning over the railing of her hospital bed to greet the baby the morning he was born. And more than twenty years later, I would be leaning over the railing of her hospital bed again to kiss her goodbye as an unsuspected brain tumor put out the brilliant light that burned inside her.

And in between, we would have a million conversations about the world. And politics. And feminism. And prostitution. As a single mother trying to put herself through graduate school, Shannon had been delighted to make friends with two prostitutes she met in the bar downstairs from the cheap Mission Street flat we shared with six other roommates.

Our conversations about sex work started the night she came home from her first shift as a call girl. I watched the baby while she was out (our family of roommates all took turns), and I worried. I was afraid for her safety, but I was also entrenched in old-school feminist ideas about prostitution and the patriarchy, and as someone who loved Shannon's new baby dearly, I worried about how this work choice would affect him. She explained to me the careful measures in place to keep her safe while she worked, how her agency was woman owned, how it functioned as a practical business staffed in large part by a surprising number of well-educated women and some men who had also made thoughtful choices about their lives.

She wanted meaningful work that would give her the freedom to finish her education and be a good mother, and this, she said, was it. And time proved that she was right. This work gave her the freedom and financial resources to have adventures with her son, Gabe Williams (who grew up to be an extraordinarily successful human being). And equally important, as she gained more experience as a sex worker, she talked about how she saw the healing aspects of what she did, how it brought touch and warmth and human connection to her clients. She, who had always loved sex, was not only able to make money doing it but also felt she was making the world a better place. In short, and contrary to everything I'd ever been conditioned to expect, it made her really happy.

Once she got her master's degree, she became an independent studies teacher in a public high school. She loved her work, both the work she did during the day and the work she continued to do at night to subsidize the miserable teacher's salary. She loved being a mother, and a friend, and a sister, a daughter, a lover, a teacher and a whore. She had the greatest capacity for true, real, big wholehearted love of anyone I have ever known. She was brave—nearly fearless.

The only time I ever saw her at less than her full electric force was after she was arrested in a sting operation and dubbed the "Teacher Prostitute" in local and then national media coverage. She lost her teaching job and found herself the butt of public jokes and primetime ridicule. It was ugly, and it made tiny cracks in what had previously been an unbreakable spirit. Robbed of the means to contribute in the ways that fed her soul, she sank lower than I'd ever seen her. But eventually she rallied because she was made of pure resilience, and she became a mentor and beloved advocate for sex workers' rights through the Sex Worker's Outreach Project and the Saint James Infirmary in San Francisco.

She got married, had two more children, became skilled in the art of legal bondage massage, loved life, lived well and died totally unexpectedly at the age of forty-eight. She left the legions of us who loved her many gifts. But for me, one of the best is that she is in every page of this book.

Because through her, and through other sex workers' advocates I met while writing about her arrest, I came to understand how dramatically the stories we choose to tell about prostitutes affect their sense of place in the world. And how historical writing about prostitution has not necessarily reflected an accurate picture so much as it has been something of a self-fulfilling prophecy, locking these women into a cycle of violent public drama.

Red Light Women of Death Valley tells the stories of women's lives, real flesh-and-blood women. They are not cautionary tales and are not meant to prove or disprove any statistical conclusion about sex work. They are presented here as testament to the extraordinary things that women can do, as witness to the extreme choices made by these women and as homage to the simple fact that they lived true lives in, around and despite whatever event brought them originally into the public eye. Some of these women were fearless, powerful and clever; some were dramatic and blustery; some made poor choices; some had bad luck; some were incredibly successful; and some were not.

As a writer, I've spent a great deal of time thinking about what it means to tell other people's stories. I think it matters that we tell each one with respect and with a willingness to connect across space and time to another's experience. But at the heart of this book is the driving need I've always felt simply to tell a good story. And these ones are fantastic. If they don't read that way, the error is in how they were written, not in how they were lived.

There's a good chance I haven't gotten every detail right or that I've missed something important. But it's time to get these women out of my hard drive and let them have their day in the sun. To them, and to Shannon, whose absence feels like a rip in the fabric of the universe, I am grateful for the way in which telling these stories expanded my heart. Because they forced me out of my comfort zone, made me think about the way I gather information and tell stories and made me reconsider what it means to honor a woman's right to control her own destiny.

Chapter 1
LOLA TRAVIS
RESPECT AND RESPECTABILITY

Inyo County, the Early Years

In the summer of 1871, a clerk at the county courthouse in Independence, California, opened a massive leather-bound book and dipped his pen in ink. Under the watchful eye of the dark-haired woman before him, he carefully copied the brands that marked a string of mules she had just purchased for $450 in gold. In thickly accented English, she gave her name for the record. He spelled it wrong, but neither of them knew the difference. Satisfied, she made her mark on the line he indicated.

It was the only entry of its kind that would appear in a volume meant to record only land transactions, but she had insisted it be made, for it proclaimed, in official ink, that the mules now belonged to her. That she couldn't read the entry was irrelevant, for she understood that it wasn't really the words that mattered; it was the official power they gave her, the power to protect her holdings and the small empire she had created.

It had been over twenty years since she came out of Chihuahua, Mexico, and into the California gold rush. In that time, she had learned to gauge the changing tides of mining camp fortunes, to read the miners—their politics, their prejudices and their weaknesses. In those years, she had watched men labor, suffer and even die as they worked to wrest their gold and silver from the earth. She had made her fortune by convincing them to put it willingly in the palm of her hand. And she had kept her fortune by understanding, in her sharp-eyed, hard-nosed way, that the Anglos revered their record books,

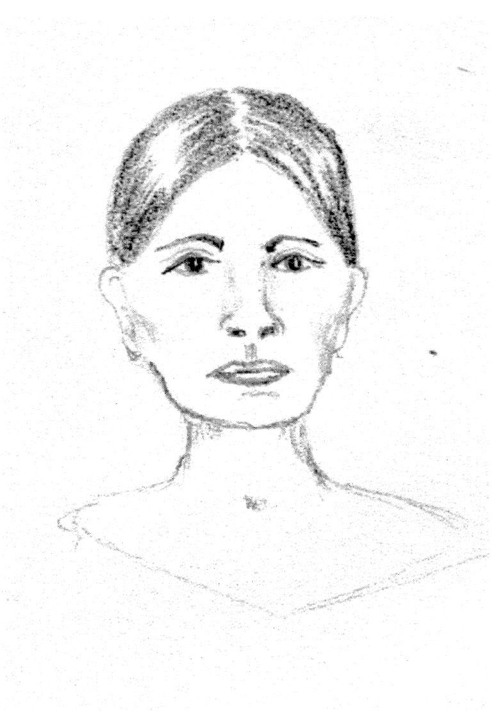

An artist's age regression portrait of Lola Travis as a young woman. *Image by Cheryl Kelsey Alvarez.*

their seals, documents, judges and officials. So she swept into the county courthouse in her fancy silk dresses, adorned with heavy gold rings and chains, to leave her mark whenever the opportunity arose.

She came quarterly to renew her liquor license, every December to pay her tax bill, every time she bought or sold a piece of property, every time she was called as a witness when another shooting occurred in one of her saloons. At thirty-four, she was one of the richest single women in Inyo County, and with her wealth she had fed and clothed, housed and educated a family dependent on her for their survival. For although she was a Mexican woman in a white man's world, she had a keen business mind, a tenacious will and a backbone of solid steel that gave her an extraordinary edge.

Her insistence on having her business transactions set down in ink not only secured her interests in an insecure world but also left a lasting and unusual record of the life of a Death Valley mining camp madam. Her name would appear in a variety of forms over the years, but she ultimately became known as Lola Travis, and that's how she has been remembered in the stories and legends of Inyo County for over 150 years.

The New California, 1850

Shortly after the Mexican-American War ended in 1848, word of the gold rush drew hopeful immigrants from Sonora and Chihuahua across the newly created border to Alta California. The territory might now technically belong to Americans, but it was still populated by Mexicans, and its wealth held the promise of a better life.

Among the hopefuls was thirteen-year-old Delores Treviso. In those days, her official footprint was indistinct, blurred by the vagaries and transience of mining camp life. The record shows a brief glimpse of her in 1850, living with two small brothers as their sole support and protection in a boardinghouse in a rough mud hole of a mining camp called Sonora in Tuolumne County. They were poor and scrambling to survive, still learning to speak English. Washing clothes on the rocks in the cold-water streams, cooking meals over an open fire—these were the things a woman could do to earn her keep. Or she could work in one of the many fandango halls where everyone—men and what few women there were—gathered in the evenings to drink, to dance and to find company.

In the early days of the California Republic, men often outnumbered women by as much as one hundred to one. Many of the Mexican women in those camps would succumb to the harsh conditions; others would find they had traded poverty and desperation at home for more of the same in a land where they were now strangers and despised by the victorious Americans. Only a few would stride into the fray, competing for resources and control of their own destinies in an arena where they were severely handicapped by their race, gender and class.

In 1851, while Lola was still struggling to survive her first years in Sonora Camp—slogging through the ankle-deep mud, dodging brawls verging on gang warfare between Anglos and Mexicans and getting used to the endless leering of lonely men—another Mexican woman named Josefa fatally stabbed a white man in the nearby town of Downieville. She had acted to defend her honor, she said, when he crashed into her shanty amid the drunken revelry of a Fourth of July celebration. The next morning, despite her desperate plea of self-defense and witnesses who were hissed off the stand during a hastily conducted lynch mob trial, she was marched to the makeshift gallows at a local bridge. There, Josefa barely had time to clear her long black hair from under the rope noose before the supports were kicked out from under her feet and she was hanged to death while a crowd of Anglos cheered.

Racial tensions were high in the days to come as Anglo and Mexican cultures clashed and more and more Anglos swelled the populations of what had been largely Mexican communities. New laws enacted by the Anglo government, including the Foreign Miners Tax, would soon marginalize the Mexican residents of California into a clearly second-class status. Coming of age in these volatile and chaotic times, Lola would hear the legends of folk heroes such as the bandits Joaquin Murietta and Tiburcio Vasquez, who mocked the interlopers and stole their gold.

In Sonora, she went to work in the fandango halls to support herself and the little boys Florentino and Martin, and she watched and learned. Her footprint remained indistinct as she grew into womanhood and romance and children occupied her thoughts. At sixteen, she became a mother, and the little girl, called Eugenia, was soon followed by a boy named Gregorio and another girl named Victoria.

Little trace of Lola appears in any official record of that time, but she continued to watch and learn and to protect and provide for her family. Then the children's father, a Mexican miner named Granillo, died, and Lola gathered her brothers, her children, her mother (who had come up from Chihuahua), her hard-earned knowledge and her innate courage and herded them all to the greener pastures of Inyo.

Death Valley, 1867

Inyo County, California, was new in 1867, having been just carved out of the edges of Mono and Tulare Counties the year before. It was composed of staggering Sierra peaks as well as the lowest, hottest, driest desert in North America. The sink of Death Valley lay not far to the east of the little foothill town of Lone Pine, a sleepy supply stop for ranchers and miners on their way to diggings elsewhere. Like most of the rest of California, it had been inhabited by Mexicans and Paiute and Shoshone Indians long before the Anglos discovered it in 1849. But unlike the gold country around Tuolumne and Sacramento, it was a somewhat forbidding land, hard to prospect, hard to work, hard to settle.

Near Lone Pine, a high mountain overlooked the Owens Lake on the very edge of the desert country. Not long after the end of the Mexican-American War, someone had named this mountain Cerro Gordo (Fat Hill), and Mexican miners had been working silver claims there on a small scale for years. But in 1865, when a man named Pablo Flores struck an unusually rich vein of silver ore, life in Inyo County, and especially on Cerro Gordo, changed forever.

Anglos came into the county in droves then, buying up Mexican diggings and staking claims of their own. In 1867, two men named Mortimer Belshaw and Victor Beaudry set up large-scale mining operations and began shipping bullion to Los Angeles, transforming that small port village into a major metropolis. At Cerro Gordo, a town sprang up around their operations, where tall smelters belched thick black smoke day and night.

Now, halfway up the steep road into town, anyone wanting admittance to that unlikely promised land was required to pay a toll. For a lone horse and rider, the outrageous fee was twenty-five cents. For a loaded wagon, the fare was one dollar.

Lola's younger brother Florentino Treviso, now a grown man, bought a mining claim and joined in the rush of hopefuls there. Since the early days in Sonora Camp, the fabric of the Treviso family had remained a tightly woven net, binding the siblings together. Now, with her own children to provide for, Lola bought a lot in Lone Pine on the rutted dirt Main Street and built a saloon. Here, as she watched over her business, shopped in the mercantile next door for whiskey and cigars and made sure her children went to school and her family was fed, she was accepted into the local community. And as she galloped down Main Street in a pair of men's pants, kicking up dust as she won a $100 horse race riding astride, the fierce and formidable Lola began to earn respect.

On another lot removed from the main thoroughfare, she established her children in a small house. Lone Pine was a relatively quiet town with a strong Hispanic community and a social hall where the important holidays of old Mexico were celebrated with all the color, noise and tradition that sojourners far from a beloved homeland could muster. It was a fine place for her family, but it was not where the real money was to be made.

In search of a more lively investment, Lola bought a lot in the new camp of Sageland in Kern County, a direct stop on the stage route from Cerro Gordo and Lone Pine to Los Angeles. She filed a homestead claim there on Main Street in 1868, but despite its robust beginnings, Sageland soon faltered. When the mines played out the following year, most of the business owners pulled up stakes and moved on. Although the Sageland venture didn't pay off, it did bring her romance in the form of a young New Englander named George Snow who kept a saloon and billiard hall near her place.

When the town died, George moved on to Cerro Gordo, and a pregnant Lola returned to Lone Pine, where she gave birth to their child, a light-skinned baby girl called Pablita who soon became the pet of her older siblings Victoria and Gregorio. That same year, at thirty-two, Lola also became a grandmother when a baby boy was born to sixteen-year-old Eugenia, who had married a miner in Havilah.

Meanwhile, Cerro Gordo was not only keeping its promise but surpassing expectations as the camp continued to grow. Sometime in 1870, Lola made her way up the Cerro Gordo Road. The tri-weekly stage from Lone Pine went at a comfortable and steady pace, but Lola, a skilled rider who always kept good stock, could easily conquer the Fat Hill grade on horseback.

Cerro Gordo wasn't a venture for the faint of heart. The steeply sloping, terraced streets were dusty in summer and muddy or snow packed in winter. Water was scarce, and hauling in materials up Belshaw's sharply pitched toll road was so expensive that the best hotel in town was constructed of flimsy frame and board. Even oxygen was scarce at such an altitude. But the landscape was not as intimidating as the men who inhabited it. The camp had quickly earned a reputation, in its remoteness, as a hideout for cutthroats and thieves. Its miners had only whiskey to console them and fistfights to relieve their tensions. Cerro Gordo was rough, violent and no place for a delicate nature, but it seemed made to order for Lola Travis.

She set up a saloon on the Main Street property claimed by George Snow, near the entrance to the big mines of Cerro Gordo. At the bottom of Main Street, a woman named Petra Romero ran a rough bordello called Waterfall's. Their two facilities stood like bookends of revelry and mayhem between which the business of a town was carried on day in and day out. Victor Beaudry's general store, claimed as payment for a debt from one of the early Mexicans on the ground, stood a stone's throw from Lola's place and offered dry goods and groceries to sober townspeople by day. Mary Morales operated a rowdy saloon across the street, and Brigida Mojardin cooked for the hungry, weary miners in her small restaurant next door. The Diaz brothers operated a billiard hall nearby, and Rosalie Salmon clanged his heavy hammer against a long succession of horseshoes in the blacksmith shop three doors down.

Early in 1871, Lola bought out George Snow's interest in the property as well as the lot next door. Here in this milieu, Lola Travis came into her own. After dark at the top of the hill, Lola's fandango hall, which included a saloon and a string of cribs out back where the prostitutes worked, presided over the camp, spilling loud music and boisterous revelers into the street at all hours of the night. Women cavorted on the dance floor and in the cribs with a steady stream of men, Hispanic and Anglo alike, who worked long, hard hours in the mines and often arrived at Lola's thirsty, lonely and unwashed, as soon as their weekly pay was in hand. But while they all came together under Lola's roof, the racial prejudice and territorial strife that had colored the new California did not recede even in this remote place, where

Inyo Independent

INDEPENDENCE, CAL.
Saturday,.........August 16, 1873

LOCAL AFFAIRS

Accidental Shooting

Monday evening last, at one of the dance houses of Cerro Gordo, occurred an accidental shooting that came near to ending the earthly career of one of the frail inmates of the institution. The partner of her joys in the dance had become superabundantly active from the effect of frequent promenades to the bar; and during his gyrations his pistol became disengaged and fell to the floor, striking, of course, on the hammer, the bullet coursing its way into the body of the frail one mentioned, inflicting a bad flesh wound. She sank to the floor but will in due time recover and "on with the dance". The episode has caused a new light to enter the head of a certain young man in regard to the proper manner of carrying fire-arms however.

something akin to street rumbles took place regularly between Anglos and Mexicans, usually erupting in either Lola's or Waterfall's and sometimes lasting for days.

Lola was a flamboyant woman, stylishly dressed, adorned with gold jewelry and armed with a pistol. She became so well known to the inhabitants of Cerro Gordo, and of Inyo County in general, that they referred to her only by her first name. When she did climb up on the more sedate stagecoach headed for the little house in Lone Pine, the driver jotted only "Lola" in his passenger log. When William Chalfant chronicled the goings-on in Cerro Gordo in his *Inyo Independent* newspaper, he frequently lamented that another shooting had occurred at "Lola's place."

Cerro Gordo was, the *Inyo Independent* declared, a "prolific source of the 'man for breakfast' order of items." Gunfire was frequent at Lola's; stray bullets nicked one of her brothers in the leg and one of her workers in the stomach and killed an old man who sat outside the saloon on a bench, minding his own business. When one of the women who earned her living in Lola's dance hall was badly beaten by a customer, the woman's boyfriend soon arrived seeking vengeance, and guns were quickly drawn and fired. A bullet "struck the woman beater in the temple, but the ball ploughed around the skull and inflicted no particular lasting damage," the *Independent*'s Chalfant reported.

On another occasion, a man "commenced to amuse himself by shooting out the lights in Lola's saloon," according to the *Independent*. Another of her customers objected to this breach of manners, drew his gun and began shooting at the first, "who returned shot for shot until both pistols were empty."

These, too, were the days when the Mexican bandit Tiburcio Vazquez rode into Inyo County and captured its imagination along with an illicit portion of its wealth. Included among the treasures he amassed were Mortimer Belshaw's pocket watch, taken in a daring 1874 stagecoach robbery not far from Cerro Gordo, as well as the boots off Belshaw's feet.

While Lola was shrewd enough to capitalize on the weaknesses of men, she was not one to give them free reign. After a particularly bloody round of gunfights in Cerro Gordo, when a civic-minded citizen visited all the businesses in town and took up a collection to build a jail, Lola and the proprietress of Waterfall's (a madam named Petra Romero, also known as Mrs. Moore) dug into their purses and handed over their contributions.

That Lola Travis and Mrs. Moore operated rival businesses seemed to create no animosity between them since, perhaps, each understood that the other walked a hard road. And despite the ongoing racial tensions, and despite her

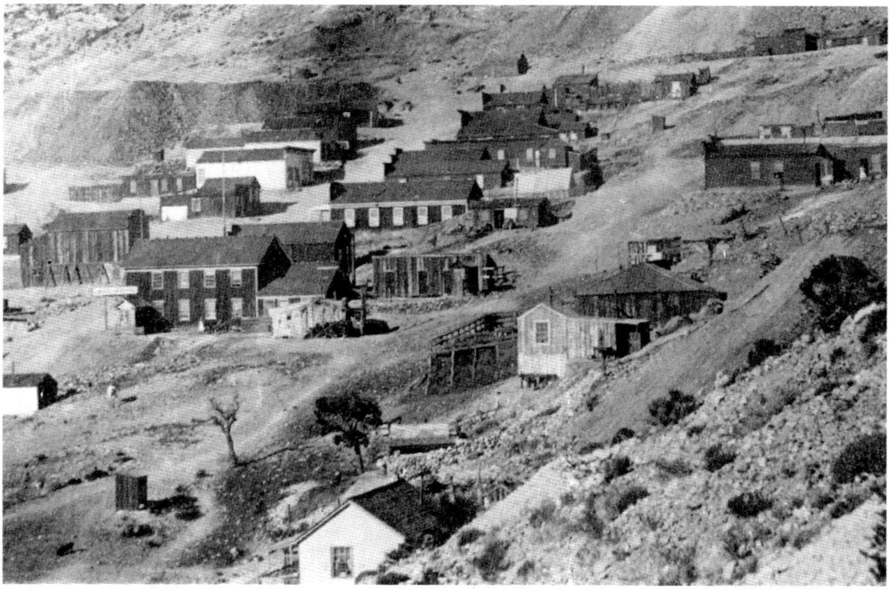

Cerro Gordo's Main Street, 1870s. *L.D. Gordon Collection, courtesy of Doug Gordon.*

own fierce temper, Lola had taken her place and maintained good working relationships with the other businesses on Main Street. In 1872, when Inyo County imposed a Sunday blue law on its saloons, Lola and Mrs. Moore banded together with John Hughes of the Cosmopolitan and K.C. Jones of the Cuckoo to buck the law and open their doors in solidarity. But by then, the long arm of the law reached all the way to Cerro Gordo, and they were hauled into court and fined between ten and fifteen dollars each.

Lola was a regular visitor at the courthouse in Independence—not usually to answer for legal infractions but to ensure that her business affairs were in order and that the official record showed her, and her alone, as the legal owner of her dominion. In time, as record keepers created a wide array of phonetic spellings, the Treviso name morphed into Travis—easier on the ears of the Anglo clerks. But while the spelling of her last name often varied, it was by her first name that she was known and recognized.

When the census enumerator visited the little house in Lone Pine in 1870 and found Lola and her children at home, he tactfully recorded her occupation as "Laundry," though Inyo County was too sparsely inhabited a place for the truth not to have been widely known. Even the soldiers at Fort Independence, some eighteen miles away in their desert garrison, knew who Lola Travis was and the nature of her business.

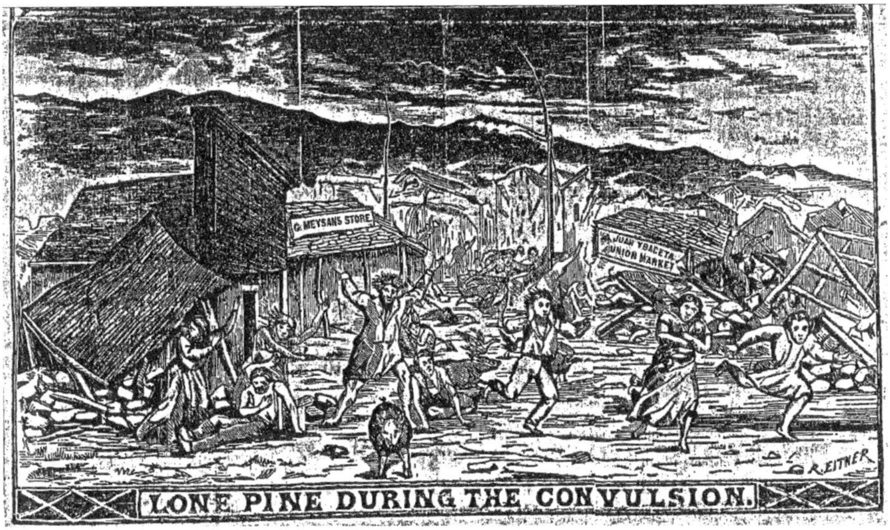

An earthquake of severe magnitude, estimated to have been a 7 or 8 on the Richter scale, struck Inyo County early on the morning of March 26, 1872, and devastated nearly the entire town of Lone Pine. Most structures in Lone Pine then were built of adobe and crumbled during the quake, killing twenty-seven people and injuring many more. Meysan rebuilt his ruined store but preserved one small segment of wall that remained standing after the quake. It still stands today behind the rebuilt structure on Main Street, encased in protective wire as the only remaining piece of very early Lone Pine architecture. *Woodcut illustrations,* San Francisco Chronicle.

If in Cerro Gordo her establishment contributed to the downfall of any number of mining camp men, in Independence her substantial taxes helped defray the resulting court and law enforcement costs.

In 1872, an earthquake opened wide fissures in the land around Lone Pine and rumbled and shook nearly every one of the town's adobe structures to the ground. Lola's saloon and the neighboring Meysan store crumbled, crushing one of Meysan's children and a young prostitute named Atonia Montoya. When the dead had been buried in a mass grave outside town, Lola and the rest of Lone Pine began rebuilding, this time with an eye to the strength and durability of their materials.

While Lola continued to preside over the Cerro Gordo venture, other members of her extended family moved into the little house in Lone Pine or into their own houses nearby. Lola's younger sister Pauline married a respected Inyo County pioneer. And in Kern County, her daughter Eugenia was raising a family and would give birth nearly once a year for the next twenty-five years.

Lola's other three children—Victoria, Gregorio and Pablita—attended school in Lone Pine, learning to speak and read and write

Inyo Independent.

INDEPENDENCE, CAL.:
Saturday,.........March 1, 1873.

LOCAL AFFAIRS.

Vamose.

During the latter part of last week, a Mexican, whose name we could not learn, came from Cerro Gordo to Lone Pine, and being tired of this country and not possessed of the necessary means to leave it, persuaded a son of Lola Trevis, a boy of thirteen, to go with him. The couple, not content to pursue their way on foot, secured two horses and a mule, the property of Lola, from Johnny Lucas' pasture; and while the Mexican, with one horse and the mule, was working about two miles below town, the boy borrowed a saddle and bridle and joined his companero. They are supposed to have taken either the road to Visalia or Los Angeles. A few days afterwards Lola despatched a Mexican after them, with a warrant, to bring the fugitives back to justice. Thus far, nothing has been heard from either party. Consequentamentally, the lovely Lola is out and injured.

English. But at home in the little house, they spoke only Spanish with their formidable and high-tempered mother. With her children, Lola was harsh, unforgiving and sometimes violent, often hitting them with enough force to leave scars that still showed in their old age. As matriarch and the force that had kept them all clothed, fed and sheltered in a world of want and hunger, she demanded their unquestioning loyalty and, for the most part, received it.

But at age thirteen, her son Gregorio, in the agonies of becoming a man, yearned to be out from under her heavy thumb. In the spring of 1873, when she was away in Cerro Gordo, Gregorio befriended an older Mexican man and formulated a plan for his escape. Together, they stole two horses and a mule from Lola's stable and rode away. As soon as she learned of his defection, Lola sent a man after Gregorio with a warrant. It was the last time he would defy her until he was much older, when he changed his name to George and moved to Arizona.

Silver Stampedes, 1874

By the fall of 1874, all of Inyo County was abuzz with the news that a new silver camp had been discovered in the Panamint Mountains. This one would surpass all others, promoters said, leaving Cerro Gordo and even the fabled Virginia City in Nevada far behind. In September, while the new camp was still only accessible by a muddy, rutted mule trail up the side of a steep canyon, Lola saddled up and rode to Panamint, becoming the first woman to purchase a piece of the rocky ground on what had been optimistically platted as a north side street. Not long after, the industrious new citizens of Panamint constructed a passable road into their "city," and other women arrived to set up shop on that same short thoroughfare. A madam named Martha Camp set up a brothel staffed by prostitutes from Virginia City, and Little Chief Street soon became better known as "Maiden Lane."

But like Sageland before it, the much-promoted Panamint fizzled quickly, and the excitement was over by the following summer, when a new camp called Darwin lured hopefuls back over the Argus Range. Lola, itching to cash in on a new town and unable by then to sell her lot in the failed Panamint, hocked her Lone Pine property for quick cash and bought a lot in Darwin in October 1875 for $150.

She was still there when a belligerent customer named Felipe Perades knocked on her door a year and a half later. He came wanting to spend the night with her, but Lola was already otherwise engaged when he arrived, and she refused his offer. His pride injured, Perades became belligerent, cursing at her that she only denied him because she liked "gringo sons of bitches" better than her own countrymen. It was an insult meant to cut deep at the heart of a proud Mexican woman, but it carried little sway with Lola. Who she liked was her own business, she answered.

Determined to get her attention, Perades produced a long stiletto blade from somewhere in his clothing and threatened to kill her with it. Lola called for the man in the next room, and Perades finally turned away. She closed her door on him, and if he had put up the knife and moved on in search of more congenial company, she might never have thought of him again.

But he didn't. Instead, Perades stood outside Lola's house that night fuming. Then, inside the front room, she moved near a lamp, and he saw the curves of her shadow cast in stark relief on the curtain. Still clutching the knife, he lunged for the silhouette at the window, shattering glass and plunging the weapon inside with murderous intent. Lola fell to the floor to avoid his arm as it stabbed about in the empty air. Then she grabbed for her own weapon, a small pistol, and ran to the door. Opening it, she took aim and fired one clean shot at Perades, hitting him in the hip.

Though the bullet hardly slowed him down at first, it burrowed deep. He was finally subdued by a local constable and led away to a friend's house, where, a miserable twenty-four hours later, he breathed his last.

The following morning, Lola stood before a jury of six white men to answer for Perades's death. They held Lola's future—and those of her children, a variety of extended family dependents and employees of her various businesses—in their hands.

But by then, she was a woman of considerable resource and presence in Inyo County. Unlike the unfortunate Josefa so many years before, her word carried weight, and on the strength of it and the testimony of the man who was already in her house that night when Perades arrived, Lola was quickly exonerated of any wrongdoing. Her plea of self-defense was accepted without question by men who knew her as a business owner and a citizen. Even the editor of Darwin's *Coso Mining News* seemed to approve of her actions and threatened that if friends of Perades attempted to seek revenge upon Lola, "the probability is that there will be more dead Mexicans."

Lola Travis was at the zenith of her red-light career. These were the days when everyone knew her by name, when her brothel in Cerro Gordo was a landmark by which the tax assessor measured the location of other property, when other women (even respectable Anglo women) envied the expensive dresses she wore. These were the days when she rode her favorite horse up and down Main Street and sometimes galloped into her saloon if she felt like it. It was her domain to do in as she pleased.

But she was a veteran of the boom and bust way of life, and she, of all people, had to have known it couldn't last. Though the mines at Darwin were still in full swing, they would soon begin to falter, and business in Cerro Gordo dwindled daily. Over the next few years, while Lola continued to travel the bandit-infested desert alone, or with young Victoria to keep her company on trips from camp to camp to oversee her little empire, more and more miners moved on to more promising ground.

George Snow had remained in Inyo County, prospecting and adventuring, and bought his own piece of property in Darwin. But he was growing restless and would soon leave Death Valley country.

By 1880, the Beaudry and Belshaw furnaces had ceased operations, and Cerro Gordo was once again the domain of the diggers and industrious Chinese who lingered to work and rework the massive tailings left behind. In March, a fire started in the kitchen at Waterfall's, long ago shut down and tamed into a residence. The children sleeping inside, apparently relatives of Doña Petra Romero, were barely pulled out before the place was consumed, and the blaze traveled up Main Street, claiming Brigida Mojardin's restaurant, the Diaz brothers' old billiard hall and, finally, Lola Travis's dance hall and residence.

For perhaps the first time in the history of the camp, every man in it came together without hesitation—Mexicans, Americans, Indians and Chinese—and pulled together to stop the blaze before it reached the far side of the street. But on Lola's side, everything burned to the foundations, leaving the small Romero children without even a pair of shoes between them. None of the owners carried insurance.

As if to add insult to injury, as her business prospects diminished that summer, a thief broke into Lola's home in Lone Pine and made off with all of her jewelry.

The following spring, Doña Lola, age forty-four, took notice of a young miner who rented a room next door to the house in Lone Pine where her children lived. During the greening and blossoming of April in the Sierras, she stood up at the courthouse in Independence and took Refugio Moreno as her lawfully wedded husband. Moreno, at twenty-three, was only a few short years older than his new stepchildren.

That year, he applied for a county liquor license for the saloon in Lone Pine, and for the first time, Lola let hers lapse. Lone Pine neither grew nor shrank and always provided a steady clientele, but slow and steady had never suited her.

As her property values declined in Inyo County, Lola prepared to begin again. All the children but Pablita were grown, and she, at fourteen, was close enough to it. Victoria was married, Gregorio was working and able to fend for himself and Lola's various siblings were now married or settled elsewhere. By 1883, Lola decided that Inyo had finally delivered all it had to offer. The Darwin and Panamint properties were worthless, and at Cerro Gordo, where she optimistically rebuilt on a small scale, there was nothing left of the boisterous camp that had made her a rich woman. After sixteen years, she sold the little house and her saloon in Lone Pine and moved on to Mojave. She left her young husband behind, being sure to specify for the record in any further business transactions that they were living "separate and apart."

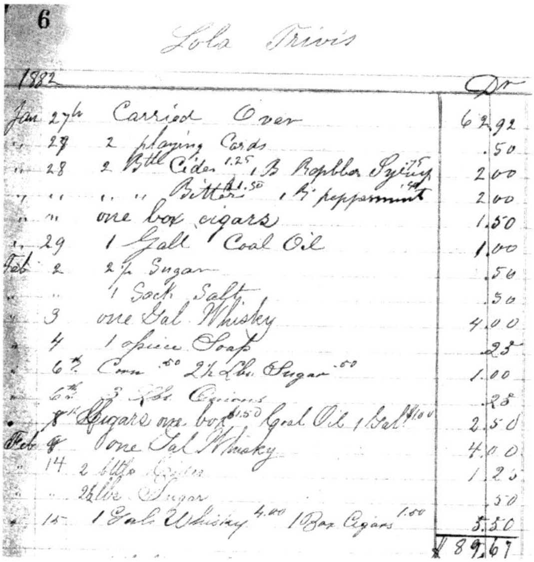
6

Lola Travis

1882		Dr
Jan 27th	Carried Over	62.92
" 27	2 playing Cards	.50
" 28	2 Btl Cider 1.25, 1 B Raspbr Syrup .75	2.00
" "	" " Bitters 1.50, 1 B peppermint .50	2.00
" "	one box cigars	1.50
" 29	1 Gall Coal Oil	1.00
Feb 2	2 lb Sugar	.50
"	1 Sack Salt	.50
" 3	one Gal Whisky	4.00
" 4	1 piece Soap	.25
" 6th	Corn .50 2½ Lbs Sugar .50	1.00
" 6th	3 Lbs Onions	.25
" 8th	Cigars one box 1.50 Coal Oil 1 Gal 1.00	2.50
Feb 9	one Gal Whisky	4.00
14	2 bttls Cider	1.25
"	2½ lbs Sugar	.50
" 15	1 Gal Whisky 4.00 1 Box Cigars 1.50	5.50
		89.67

A page from Lola Travis's account at the Meysan General Store in Lone Pine, showing her purchases from February through March 1882. The list includes bottles of cider and syrup, whiskey by the gallon, limes, pickles, cheese, soap, coal oil, claret and cigars. Other items on her store account included playing cards, peppermint, onions and salt, as well as dress goods and lace in blue and black. Food items, presumably purchased to feed the family, appeared on her daughter Victoria Otero's store account. Charles Meysan also acted as Lola's agent and collected rents from her various properties after she moved to Mojave. *Courtesy of Eastern California Museum.*

In Mojave, fierce winds blew a never-ending hail of sand and hats snatched from the heads of careless men across the Southern Pacific Railroad tracks. But women were still scarce, and the railroad, along with the newly built gargantuan twenty-mule team wagons hauling borax out of Death Valley, provided regular business. Here, for a change, things were booming.

Kern County, 1884

In 1884, the Southern Pacific Railroad brought thirty-one-year-old Thomas Cronin to Mojave, working as a supervisor for the desert outpost. Born in County Cork, Ireland, he had come into the country as a child and farmed with his family until the romance, and more reliable pay, of the railroad lured him away. He had worked his way up from section hand to supervisor. That August, in the already terrible heat of summer, when an explosion in the railroad's roundhouse started a wildfire that burned most everything in Mojave to the ground, it would have fallen to him to deal with the aftermath. Among those affected by the fire was Doña Lola Moreno, who, when it suited her purposes, identified herself as a Spanish widow. Doña Lola soon relocated, with her usual force of will, to Tehachapi, but the Southern Pacific stopped there, too, and she and Cronin would cross paths again.

In the fall of 1889, they were married in Los Angeles, and he went back to farming on a 437-acre ranch in Cummings Valley outside Tehachapi, with forty head of cattle and twenty horses. Thirteen years her junior, Thomas Cronin was small statured and thin, only four and a half feet tall, while Lola had thickened with age and begun wearing only dour black dresses. He was good natured and easygoing; her temper had only worsened as time passed. With her children gone, Thomas became the object of her wrath, and when he was unlucky enough to trip the delicate trigger of her temper, Lola picked him up bodily and set him down on the hot surface of her cook stove, burning his backside.

But Thomas Cronin was the bridge between Doña Lola and the one thing she had not attained on her own. Despite the fact that she had earned her fortune on the far side of the moral dividing line between public women and polite society, she had overcome moral and racial prejudice and managed to command respect. But it was only later, as the "widow" who married dependable, respectable Thomas Cronin, that she attained respectability.

In 1892, Thomas was profiled in a biographical history of Kern County as "one of a class of men whose individual labors have contributed materially to the growth and advancement of Central California." As his wife, Lola's name also appeared in this impressive book. The following year, the couple stood as sponsors at the baptism of Eugenia's daughter Maria Concepcion at the Catholic church in Tehachapi. The Treviso family remained tightly knit, and Lola's younger brother Martin lived with the Cronins on their farm, while Pablita and Eugenia also settled in Kern County.

Together, Lola and Thomas Cronin bought and sold a great deal of property in Kern County, and parcels were frequently traded back and forth between Lola and her children. In 1900, Lola, having given up the pursuit of miners, now turned to mining. She and Thomas went into partnership with several other associates and formed the San Antonio Mining and Mill Company.

Lola Travis Moreno Cronin had marched full force into respectability.

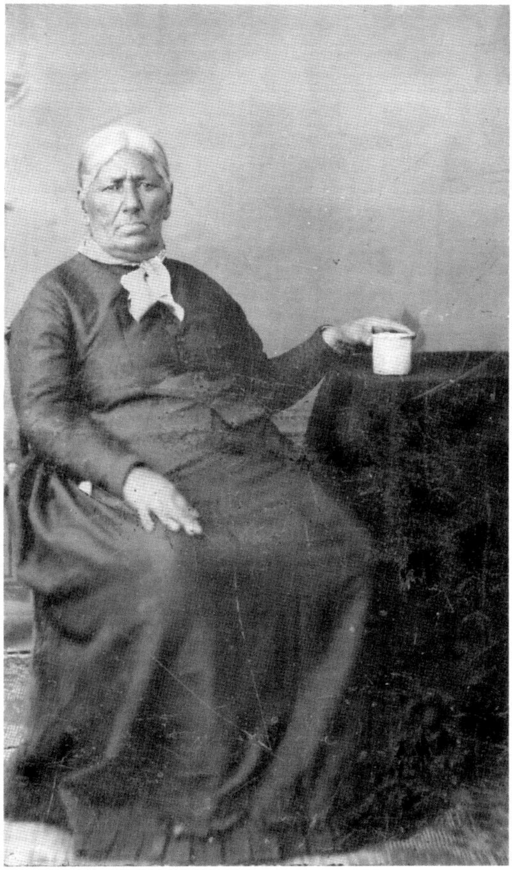

Delores "Lola" Travis Moreno Cronin as an old woman, around the turn of the century in Bakersfield. *Courtesy of Lola Gillespie Miller and Gillespie/Miller family.*

Epilogue

In about 1911, as Lola began to show her age, the Cronins moved from the Cummings Valley ranch into a house on Fremont Street in Bakersfield, where Thomas worked as a teamster for Sandstone Brick and Lola lived for the first time since coming to California in an established city with paved streets.

On November 13, 1912, a headline on the front page of the *Bakersfield Californian* read, "One of County's Oldest Women Is Dead." At seventy-five, Lola Cronin's long life ended when a tumor burst in her throat. The writer of the obituary included only a few sparse details of Lola's life, and those, as given by her daughter Eugenia Rios, were largely fabricated to erase a past Lola's children still struggled to live down. The obituary contained none of the effusive sentiment often lavished on the pioneers of young mining camps who came into the country early and staked their futures on it. Its faint praise was grudging, but Lola's passing had nonetheless merited a front-page story.

At the time of her death, Lola's personal property consisted of three dozen chickens, a horse, one gold bracelet and a coral bead chain. These material possessions seemed pitifully small compared to the wealth she had once amassed, but her legacy would ultimately not be counted in material things. In Bakersfield, where she had settled as an already old woman, Lola was remembered as a pioneer. Her four children produced some thirty grandchildren, and they produced many more children of their own. Today, her great-grandchildren, one of whom was named Lola, still live in California and recount bawdy stories about Doña Lola's dance halls and saloons.

Despite the well-known reputation of their mother, Lola's daughters never followed her into the brothel profession. In fact, it seems clear she was determined that they do just the opposite. Like Eugenia, Victoria married young to a miner in Independence. After bearing several children, she fled her abusive husband and never remarried. Victoria lived for a time in Arizona and then ran a rooming house in Jackson, California, where prostitutes with short hair and bright lipstick sometimes attended the dances on Saturday nights. But they came as independent workers, not employed by Victoria, who cooked the food, scrubbed the floors and did the miners' laundry to get them ready for these dances but drew the line at procuring their dates. At some point in her life, Victoria also spent time with her relatives in Chihuahua, where family legend tells that she befriended the younger sister of legendary Mexican revolutionary Pancho Villa.

Eugenia's first husband (who was twenty-two years her senior) died, and she later remarried a Chilean man named Miguel Vega. She spent many years with Vega, and the union produced at least eleven children. After his death, she married Manual Rios, a gardener by trade, and settled in Bakersfield. She appears to have led a quiet life as a housewife and once estimated for the census that she had given birth to a total of twenty-two children, many of whom did not survive.

Pablita married a wealthy man and became a society matron.

The only one of Lola's children who did go into the business was George, who reportedly ran a Prohibition-era speakeasy and brothel in Stockton, California.

High on the mountain at Cerro Gordo, the last remnant of Lola's old cribs still stands, listing and splintering in the wind and rain and sun. Today, over 130 years later, some of the surviving stories visitors tell here even include what the interior of Lola's dance hall looked like—that she had a crescent moon and stars carved into the wooden ceiling. Over the years, pieces of her crumbling cribs were carried off by enthusiasts, and they are now stashed away in homes across the country.

In no other part of Death Valley has a legend quite like this one survived, but the stories that remain only capture a small moment of Lola Travis's history—the moment in which as a rowdy madam of the Old West she carried a gun and had to lift her skirts to walk across her own dance floor without dragging them through the blood of one of her customers.

But underneath the hyperbole of the legend was a flesh-and-blood woman whose life was so much more than that—whose choices carried a price and upon whose strength of will the lives of smaller, younger, weaker family members depended.

Lola Travis was never remembered as kind. But it had probably not been her intention to be kind. Most likely, it was her intention to survive and then to prosper and finally to win respect. In the midst of the political transformation of California, in a time of easy hatred and casual violence that had defeated many a weaker soul, Doña Lola was transformed and emerged from the fray victorious.

Chapter 2
CERRO GORDO'S MAIN STREET AFTER DARK

It would have been cold in Cerro Gordo just before sunrise on the morning of January 22, 1872, despite the Beaudry and Belshaw smelting furnaces belching smoke nearby. Most of the businesses in town would still have been closed at such an early hour, waiting for the shopkeepers, cooks, clerks, washerwomen and hostlers to haul themselves out of bed and get on with their work.

But while the rest of the town prepared to rise and meet the new day, the inhabitants of the rowdy Main Street dance halls were just winding down another long night. At Lola Travis's place on the high end of town, the girls were still shuffling around the floor with a few die-hard customers. On the lower end, poised to be the first to catch thirsty, lonely miners as they clambered into town, stood a rough dance hall called Waterfall's. The proprietress, known as Madam Moore, was just retiring with Rosealtis Garcia, her last customer for the night. Waterfall's made no claim to elegance, and even the madam worked in a bare room with only a mattress on the floor.

Around 5:00 a.m. on this particular night, a Mexican man named Sabine Alvarez came in to Lola's, danced a few dances and left with his friend Jose Barrega, headed down Main Street toward Waterfall's.

There Alvarez rattled the knob on Moore's door, saying he wanted to come in and take a drink while his friend Barrega, who was quite drunk, fell down in the street. Moore, otherwise occupied, called for him to refrain from insulting her or her house. Alvarez responded that he hadn't meant to insult anyone. At this point, Barrega suggested to his friend that they leave, but it was too late. The door opened, a pistol barked and Alvarez fell in the dust beside his companion, shot through the left breast.

Alvarez managed to make his way back up Main Street to Lola's, where he told her he'd been shot and asked her to loan him a pistol. Clearly, however, he was in no shape to use it. Lola made him as comfortable as she could in a bed in one of her rooms, where he died within the hour attended by the local doctor.

Garcia was held briefly for questioning and then fled Inyo County and never stood to answer for his crime. But this incident provides one of the few unintentional glimpses into the lives of the dance hall women on Fat Hill. Despite the fact that the camp was nearly five years old and had known plenty of violence and mayhem already, this was the one of the first dramatic killings in its history, and the *Inyo Independent* carefully reported the proceedings of the coroner's inquest.

The situation in Cerro Gordo is unique in the history of the Death Valley camps for several reasons. In addition to Lola Travis, whose tenure in Cerro Gordo is well documented, records suggest that a good portion of the night business on Main Street was controlled by Hispanic women. The Madam Moore who shared a room with Rosealtis Garcia on the night he shot Sabine Alvarez was actually a Mexican woman named Petra Romero.

Romero was thirty-two in 1870 when the census enumerator found her living in Cerro Gordo. She reported a personal wealth of $200, more than the average single woman of her time, and the following year, she purchased the property believed to be Waterfall's dance hall for $150. Whether the previous operator might have been someone named Maggie Moore and Romero simply continued to use the name, or whether she assumed the surname of Moore for the sake of convenience is unknown. Over the next three years, Romero built up her business, and in 1874, she capitalized on her investment when she sold the property to another woman for $3,000, including all beds and bedding.

If Lola's place was the scene of many violent encounters, Romero's was only slightly behind as these establishments, offering the only source of comfort for lonely, edgy and sometimes disillusioned and frustrated men, attracted the roughest elements of the camp. In between Romero's place and Lola Travis's saloon, there were several other businesses operated by Hispanic women, including Mary Morales's saloon, which was across the street from Lola's and employed at least one male bartender. Morales bought her property in 1872 and paid taxes on it until 1879, though she sold part of the lot to saloonkeeper Antonio Moreno in 1876.

Brigida Mojardin, who also owned a house near Lola's in Lone Pine, bought a lot behind Lola's dance hall and ran a restaurant there. Mojardin continued to pay her taxes even after her place was consumed by the fire of 1880.

Concepcion Flores purchased Petra Romero's property in 1874 and continued to run it for several years. Concepcion and her mother, Guadalupe, may have been related to Romero, or the two had close ties of some kind since Guadalupe was living with Romero when the 1870 census enumerator came to call. The Floreses also owned a ranch outside Lone Pine and several local mining claims. Guadalupe is one of the few Mexican residents of Inyo County at that time who applied to become a naturalized citizen of the United States. She and Lola also held county-issued liquor licenses in Cerro Gordo up until the 1880 fire.

A woman named Josefa Pine held and paid taxes on a Main Street lot near Lola's saloon. In addition to these business ventures, Hispanic women also held several mining claims in the area.

A study of the surviving records indicates a kind of close-knit solidarity among these women, who often lived and worked near to one another. They sometimes even paid their taxes on the same day, as if perhaps one of their number gathered everyone's payments and delivered them when she traveled down the hill and over to the courthouse at Independence.

It is also interesting to note that a good third or fourth of all merchants licensed to sell liquor in Inyo County were women during the 1870s. However, by the mid-1880s, when the Cerro Gordo, Darwin and Panamint booms were over, not one woman held a county liquor license.

While most surviving records show a predominance of Hispanic women, they were not the only ones who worked in the Cerro Gordo dance halls. May Merritt, an Irish woman with a deep sentimental attachment to her homeland, was known as "The Fenian" in Cerro Gordo and Lone Pine, where fighting and drinking were her favorite pastimes. She took especial offense at anyone who impugned Ireland or the insurgent Irish brotherhood called the Fenians. Legend has it that Merritt always traveled with a large black dog and enjoyed a good fistfight.

While these women owned their own businesses, and therefore in large measure controlled their own destinies, or operated as free agents like the Fenian, the other end of the spectrum was also represented in Cerro Gordo. Chinese slave prostitutes were in the camp as early as 1872, according to one article in the *Inyo Independent*. The Chinese community was a significant portion of the population there and remained so until the end of the camp. Chinese women were still arriving on the stage in 1877.

The Fenian of Cerro Gordo—Memories of Dr. Hugh K. McClelland

The Fenian, a beautiful Irish girl with eyes of blue, was the reigning belle of the camp. Her besetting sin was drink, and at times she lost all control of herself, which exacted pity as she was a great big-hearted woman and did many acts of charity to those in sickness and financial distress.

I seldom visited the dance halls except in cases when someone was shot or cut, which was of frequent occurrence. The dance hall girls, mostly Mexicans, all had fictitious names, and very odd ones, I can tell you. The Horned Toad, a fiery, high-tempered Mexican girl, was on the floor cutting some high and fantastic stunts and a young man asked me her name. I told him she was the Horned Toad, and she overheard me and came at me like a flash with a stiletto drawn and would have plunged in into me had not the Fenian caught her by the wrist. The Horned Toad disliked the name given her very much and was ready at all times to fight, and especially when under the influence of liquor.

A Mexican who was a friend of hers came running toward me with a knife in his hand, and George Snow, who saw that something serious might happen to me, shot the Mexican dead. This resulted in a general shooting, and the lights were extinguished at once. The hall became filled with powder smoke, and pandemonium reigned among those present.

Cerro Gordo was located on the mountain, and many houses were built on the hillsides, with terraced walks or paths leading close to the roofs of cottages just beneath. One starry night when the Fenian had on a large cargo of whiskey, she went for a stroll along one of the paths, lost her footing and fell through the roof of a shack below, where ten or twelve Chinamen were seated at a table playing tan, and lighted on the center of the table. The commotion and sudden fright of the Chinamen can well be imagined. One of the Chinamen in his hurried exit fell over an embankment and broke his leg.

There is some indication that Lola Travis procured women from other cities to work in her brothels and dance halls rather than depending on fate to bring them to her doorstep. When noted true crime writer John Gilmore spent time in the ghost town of Cerro Gordo in the 1970s, he was told an interesting story by the town's then owner. The story was supported by a photograph and an old diary (which disappeared after the owner's death), from which Gilmore made a few sparse notes, and concerned the fate of a prostitute named Rosanna Murdoch. Murdoch was believed to have worked on San Francisco's Barbary Coast until she was imported to Cerro Gordo by Lola Travis through some kind of procurement network. Rosanna worked in Cerro Gordo for perhaps a year or two and later is believed to have moved on to Tombstone. The story suggested that Rosanna had not come into the profession of her own free will.

By the mid-1870s, the camp was foundering, its population was declining and its social makeup was far more tame. In 1876, a brief attempt to revive Cerro Gordo resulted in another shooting affray when some of the remaining townspeople held a New Year's Day ball in an abandoned dance hall (probably Romero's) and the revelry got out of hand. Shortly thereafter, a letter appeared in the *Inyo Independent* complaining that the paper "could so far forget all principles of decency as to dare call that ball a 'hurdy gurdy dance'—and to have the impudence to brand nearly every respectable woman in the place, married or single, as a 'prostitute.' It is true the ball took place in a hall formerly used as a dance house; but…on this particular occasion not a woman of disreputable character was present, the rule for their exclusion having been rigidly and effectually enforced."

The 1880 fire that wiped out Waterfall's, Lola Travis's and everything in between put an end to any hopes for a real rejuvenation of the night life in Cerro Gordo. However, the camp saw brief revivals over the years, and as late as World War II, a stand of old cribs on the site of Lola's old dance hall was reported to have housed women who catered to the soldiers living on the hill.

Chapter 3

MURDER, MAYHEM AND MARTHA CAMP

PANAMINT CITY, 1874

Sometime in the early winter of 1874, the Panamint and Lone Pine stage, laboring under the weight of its much-anticipated cargo, lumbered up the precipitous grade of Surprise Canyon, then little more than a deep notch cleft into a mountain overlooking the Death Valley desert. Inside the coach, legend has it, was the big, buxom Martha Camp, late of Virginia City, traveling with some of the finest Comstock prostitutes she could recruit for the venture. They would be among the first women to arrive in the new camp of Panamint, where, until recently, men had been sleeping in caves or on the ground and the terrain was so steep and treacherous that no wheeled conveyance could navigate it.

Like the famed Virginia City before it, Panamint had attached itself to the inhospitable side of an isolated mountain range. But many of Virginia's best mining men had staked their faith and pledged their fortunes on the belief that this mountain was packed with rich silver ore. Having already carved great wealth out of the Comstock lode, they were confident they could do the same at Panamint. The hopefuls came from all corners of the American West and the world, with European, Chinese and Mexican immigrants all represented in the stampede.

For most of the estimated seven hundred men already on the ground that fall, the new camp was a gamble at long odds. Few would turn out to possess either the luck or the skill to locate a silver claim capable of turning their

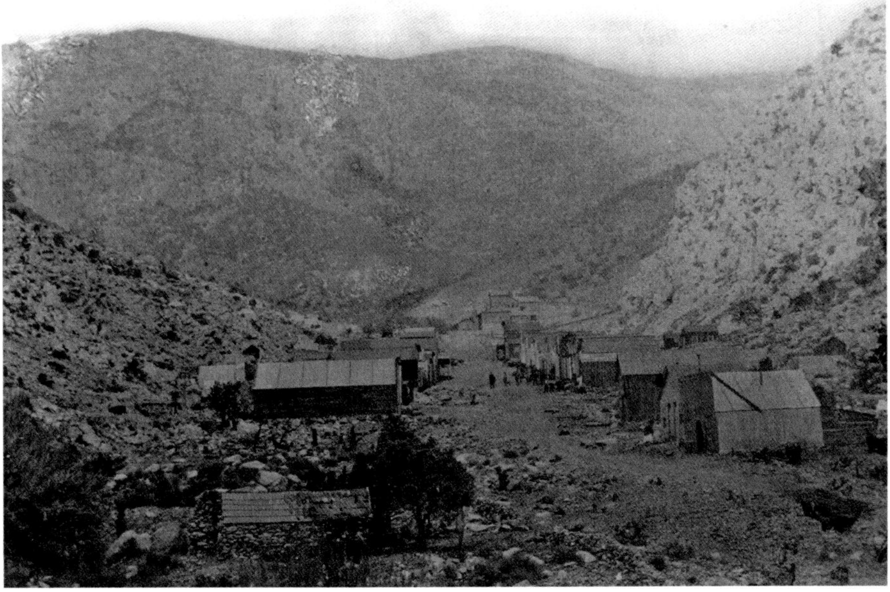

Panamint City, circa 1875. *Courtesy of Easter California Museum.*

rich dreams into reality. A far better gamble was made by those who followed the stampede, trundling up the mountain with wagonloads of groceries, restaurant outfits or the furnishings of a boardinghouse or saloon. Those most likely to succeed were the women who came to cash in on the loneliness of men surrounded by nothing but tall mountains, hard ground and other men.

While Martha Camp had to have understood that hardship would be a part of the equation at Panamint, the wide-open freedom of the rough camp and the sheer possibility represented by its very newness might have been enough to make the inconveniences worthwhile. By 1874, the fifteen-year-old camp of Virginia City had been civilized into a town with rules and regulations built on a foundation of Victorian morals and manners that left little room for prostitutes. Martha had spent ten years on the Comstock, watching the social sphere of prostitutes narrow to the point that the lure of a hardscrabble camp was preferable to the stodginess of a town with all the amenities.

Every new camp was a risk, but the newness held promise that lured the aspirants forward, fueled by hope and hyperbole until the veins played out and the excitement was over. Some, like a man named Horace B. Camp, would stand at the very threshold of enormous wealth. He claimed a stake in the fabulous Yellow Jacket mine in the very early days of Virginia City but died penniless less than a decade later, leaving his young wife to navigate an uncertain future on her own.

Virginia City, 1859

Virginia City in 1859 was little more than a collection of tents clinging to the side of a mountain, but word of the fabulous silver ledge discovered by Henry Comstock that summer brought hopefuls to the new camp by the thousands. The rich silver of the Comstock lode changed the American West, earned statehood for Nevada and even influenced the outcome of the Civil War. And all along its edges, thousands of smaller tales of heartbreak and triumph played out as the years went by. Some men got rich and then got richer. Others got rich and then got poorer.

Horace B. Camp had, for a brief twenty-four hours, held title to a share in Comstock's Ophir mine—the one that would later produce millions of dollars in silver ore. But Henry Comstock, in a fit of depression, had sold it to Camp for only a dollar down. The following morning, Comstock's friends marched Camp to a makeshift justice court and demanded that he return his interest.

Camp then set about staking as many claims in the vicinity of the Ophir as he legally could. One of these, named the Yellow Jacket, would be among the most important Virginia mines for years to come, and Camp became an important mining man.

By 1864, the city had grown, settled and begun to refine its social and civic infrastructure, providing a small selection of marriageable young women. That February, in the rector's study of the newly formed St. John's Episcopal Church, Horace joined himself in matrimony to a large and powerfully built twenty-one-year-old Irish girl named Martha Margaret Dickey.

Martha had already survived the Great Hunger in Ireland that killed one million or more people—an eighth of that small country's entire population. Two million more, with a young Martha among their number, fled Ireland in over-packed, under-stocked freight ships bound for America. Whatever their pre-famine circumstances might have been, by the time most Great Hunger refugees arrived in America, they had little more than the clothes on their backs. Most landed on the East Coast of the United States and settled in one of the already overcrowded boroughs of New York City.

By the time Martha was in her early twenties, the East Coast was in the desperate throes of the American Civil War. But out West, in places like the fabulous new silver camp of Virginia City, Nevada, the sky and the possibilities were limitless. Many young Irish women migrated to the western mining camps seeking domestic service jobs, and homes and husbands as well.

Martha may have felt quite pleased with her future prospects in marrying the successful Camp, but within two years, the Yellow Jacket suffered a severe decline, went into receivership and was taken over by a notorious mining magnate named William Sharon. The Camps then ran a small saloon in what was probably also their residence on C Street until H.B. died a short time later, leaving young Martha to fend for herself. With her husband gone, she made the radical decision to begin working as a prostitute. She also sold drinks to augment her income and identified herself as a saloonkeeper in the city directory.

She soon came to know many of the inhabitants of Virginia City's Barbary Coast neighborhood (named after the San Francisco Barbary Coast prostitution district), as well as many other women of the demimonde. Among the friends she made in her new life was a woman named Julia Bulette.

Virginia City, 1867

Late on the night of May 3, 1867, the wind howled along Virginia City's South C Street, forcing itself in through the cracks of a two-room frame cottage where Martha Camp lay sleeping. Martha was twenty-five and lived and worked alone in her small house. Her establishment competed with a variety of other saloons and cribs ranging along South C Street, offering the services of women from just about every corner of the world.

Earlier in the evening, the music, shouting and noise of hundreds of pairs of heavy feet stumbling through the crowded dirt streets outside filled the night air. Now, in the hours just before dawn, it was quiet enough that the sound of rustling silk woke Martha from her sleep. At first, she thought it must be the fierce wind ruffling some dresses hanging near her bed. But as she lay listening, she soon distinguished another noise, as if a man were creeping along the floor, dragging the toes of his shoes. The sound of it struck fear in her heart.

On the Comstock's Barbary Coast that year, the notion that a man might skulk into a prostitute's room late at night with malicious, rather than lascivious, intent wasn't at all farfetched. Only five months before, Julia Bulette, one of the more genteel and well liked of the Virginia City demimonde, had been found murdered in her own bed. She had been beaten, strangled and suffocated by a desperate and determined hand, an unknown killer who left no clues behind. In the wake of the crime, rumors of similar killings in San Francisco left Comstock prostitutes on edge, even as sixteen carriages full of them followed Julia's body to the graveyard in the midst of a bitter winter storm.

It wasn't that violence against prostitutes on the Comstock was unusual. Before her own death, Julia testified at the trial of a man who had beaten her friend Lizzie Hayes to within an inch of her life. But as a general rule, this sort of violence wasn't perpetrated by unknown assailants, and when it was extreme, it did not go unpunished. Julia's testimony helped to convict Lizzie's attacker and send him to the state penitentiary. But after Julia's death, no witnesses came forward—no one had seen the killer slip into her small house in the dark hours of night or out of it again as a watery cold dawn broke over steeply sloping D Street.

Violence and mayhem were simply a part of mining camp life, especially for women who lived and worked in the red-light districts, outside the protections of polite society, where alcohol flowed freely and emotions often ran rampant. But what happened to Julia was different. It seemed especially vicious and brutal in a community where vicious and brutal were standard fare. But worse, it left so many questions unanswered, such as who had done it, and why?

An uneasiness lingered still on that May night nearly four months later when Martha raised herself up to look around her room and saw, crouching behind the bed, a man with a dagger in his hand. She leaped up, screaming for help as she ran for the door, and burst onto C Street in her nightclothes. Even at that late hour, there were plenty of people about, and they quickly converged on Martha's room, where they found only a cudgel on the floor and the back door hanging open.

By morning, word had spread about the attack, and even the *Daily Trespass* reporter couldn't help but speculate that Julia's murderer had tried to kill again. In those days, the term "serial killer" had yet to be invented, but the prostitutes on C and D Streets had imagination enough to conjure up a man bent on robbing and killing more of their number.

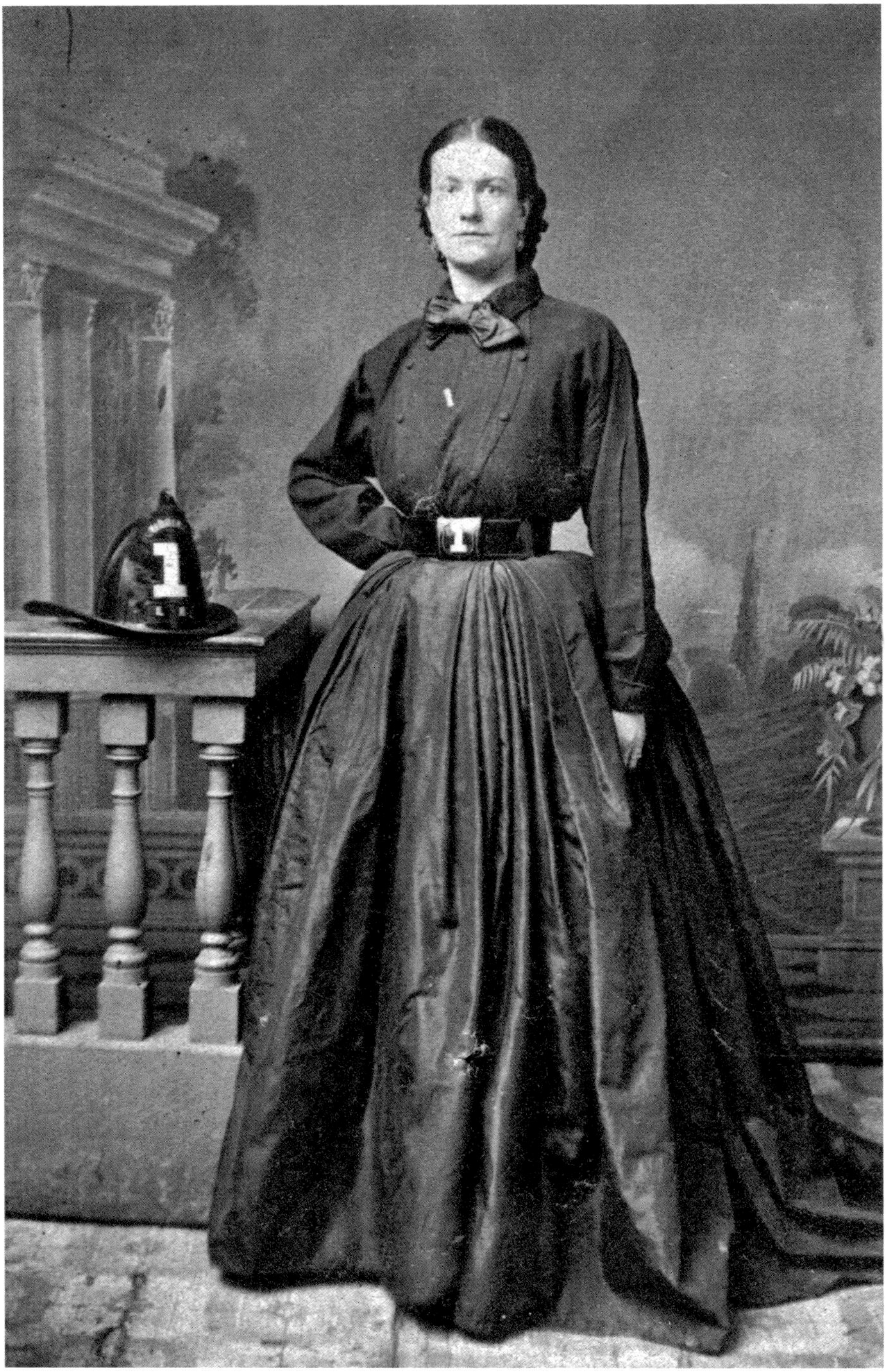

Julia Bulette in her honorary fireman's uniform, circa 1866. *Courtesy of Nevada State Historical Society.*

At the time of her death, Julia Bulette was as close to an upstanding, respectable citizen as a woman in her socio-political context could be. She lived in a modest but well-furnished cottage within the legal limits of the red-light district. She went to the theater and the opera and attended grand "whore" balls. She was well liked by her female friends, one of whom considered her "like a sister" and trusted her with a packet of diamonds. She referred to her customers as friends and was well thought of by men like Alfred Doten, a journalist with the *Territorial Enterprise* newspaper. The local fire department was so grateful for her financial support that it made her an honorary member.

"She was thirty five years of age, belonging to that class denominated 'fair but frail,'" reported the *Territorial Enterprise* after her murder, "yet being of a very kind-hearted, liberal, benevolent and charitable disposition, few of her class had more true friends."

And still, she had been murdered in her own bed.

Jewelry and furs were taken from her room, but this didn't account for the sheer brutality of the crime and did little to calm the unease of others who feared they might meet the same fate.

Julia's body had been found by her friend Mary Jane Minere, who had come to fetch her for the breakfast they shared every morning. Minere, who also worked as a prostitute, had been named as executrix of Julia's estate, and she and other women who worked on D and C Streets pledged a reward for the killer. A quick and rather haphazard arrest was made soon after the murder, but the suspect was released on the strength of his alibi. From then until that May, the unanswered questions hovered in the air over the Comstock tenderloin.

On the morning after Martha was attacked, the *Daily Trespass* regretted that she hadn't gotten a good look at her attacker's face. Nothing more was said of the event until ten days later, when Martha changed her mind and declared that not only had she seen him that night, but she had seen him again on the street and could identify him.

> The prostitutes of Virginia City were much more genteel and sophisticated in their attempts to bring Julia Bulette's killer to justice than a group of their sisters in Las Animas, Colorado, in 1874. That year, when a man killed prostitute Lizzie Allen with a rock because he said she owed him a dollar, the prostitutes formed a vigilante committee and hanged him from a tree.

A French immigrant named John Millain (whose full and actual name, he said, was Jean Marie A Villain) was promptly arrested and charged with attempting to commit burglary. Before he could stand trial for that crime, however, a shopkeeper came forward and identified him as the man who had sold her one of the dresses stolen from Julia's cottage. More of Julia's things were found in a trunk he had stored away, and authorities had enough circumstantial evidence to charge him with the crime. The other charges against him were never prosecuted.

Millain was eventually convicted of the murder, and the C Street scare was over. "That John Millain is the cruelest and most heartless murderer of the age is beyond doubt," the *News* reported. "His last deed, it is supposed, is only the conclusion of a series of crimes perpetrated on women that makes the blood run cold with horror to contemplate. That he has been a professional strangler there is but little doubt, and his last confession will doubtless elucidate the terrible doubts that have shrouded several murders in California with impenetrable mystery."

The hoped-for confession, however, never materialized, and Millain adamantly insisted that he was not guilty of anything more than receiving stolen property from a couple of casual acquaintances.

For Martha, there was little peace of mind to be found in Millain's conviction. She had not been called to testify against him, the charge of burglary having been set aside until the matter of the Bulette killing could be sorted out. It was, perhaps, kept in reserve in case the prosecution failed to win its conviction or the subsequent appeal.

That October 1867, while the appeal was still pending, Martha sat alone one afternoon in the back room of her cottage, sewing, when a man she didn't know came in and asked for a drink. She led him to the bar in her sitting room and sold him a glass of wine, but then suddenly he lunged at her, wrapped his hands around her throat and swore that he would kill her. Martha fought him off but was considerably shaken.

It was not the first time since Julia's murder she had been threatened, she told the *Daily Enterprise* later, exhibiting the scratches and bruises at her neck for the reporter's inspection. Although Millain had already been convicted, Martha declared she stood ready to testify against him if she should be called at his appeal. This, she was convinced, was the reason for the threats.

Millain's conviction held, and he swung to his death at the end of a rope at Virginia City's first hanging in April 1868, but not before he again declared his innocence and deplored the fact that he had been convicted by the testimony of "public women" whose "licentious looks" contributed to his condemnation. "In Virginia City," he said, "the public women are more respected than honest ladies." The most damning evidence against him at the trial was given by other prostitutes who, when shown the stolen flounced silk and more demure plaid gowns found in Millain's possession, identified them as having been worn by Julia.

Although Martha never got the chance to testify against Millain in court, it was common knowledge that she had identified him as the man in her room the year before, and this had prejudiced the entire town against him. Even Mark Twain, who attended the hanging of Millain, cited his attack on Martha as evidence of his desperate character and that he "was no common murderer…he was a heartless assassin."

Despite the fact that Millain's death removed him as a potential threat, Martha had apparently grown weary of living alone and unprotected. By 1870, she had moved into rooms attached to a C Street saloon owned by a Norwegian couple named George and Louisa Olffen and was sharing quarters with four other prostitutes. Among her roommates at Olffen's was Mercedes Navarro, a well-to-do Chilean madam who later ran a house at 10 C Street. Navarro was a great friend of *Territorial Enterprise* reporter Alfred Doten.

The early 1870s were difficult times for Virginia City's "women of the town." Several fires ravaged D Street, some perhaps deliberately set, pushing some prostitutes out of the legally sanctioned red-light district and into the rest of the city. The crib occupied by Julia Bulette, among many others, was swallowed up in the blazes.

If Millain's complaint that prostitutes in Virginia City were held in high esteem had been true at the time of his death, the tide of public opinion was turning. In early 1874, Virginia and Truckee Railroad officials unceremoniously evicted several women from their quarters near D and Union Streets. Meanwhile, the town aldermen began regular discussions about stricter regulation or even abolition of the prostitution trade within the city.

Attempts to pass strongly worded ordinances failed, but Martha apparently could feel the walls closing in. Virginia was nearly fifteen years old and struggling to recover from an economic slump. Neither circumstance boded well for prostitutes.

Panamint City, 1874

News of a promising silver strike in a remote California camp on the edge of Death Valley soon captured Martha's imagination. Though the *Territorial Enterprise* warned hopefuls about pulling up stakes for Panamint just as the Comstock was experiencing a revival, Martha paid no attention. Virginia City was abuzz with the news of the strike, and it was said that the men of Panamint, lacking the appropriate facilities in that camp, were traveling all the way to San Francisco to spend their hard-earned silver in brothels there.

"Tents of cloth and poles, huts of rock, and shanties of bark adorn the place," read a report of Panamint in the *Territorial Enterprise* on November 19. "Many of the inhabitants live in tunnels and natural cavities in the rocks…A great scarcity of eating and lodging houses prevails; one is satisfied to sleep in a corral, and a dish of bacon and beans with a potato thrown in sometimes is a meal not to be sneezed at."

The paper cautioned that all of the good prospects had already been claimed and "not one in ten…at Panamint will make money."

But Martha had good reason to believe that if she gambled on the venture, she would be among the lucky 10 percent. One San Francisco madam recalled that the men were rolling into that city from Panamint with their pockets full of money and "steam coming from their ears."

As the geographic and social sphere of prostitutes narrowed on the Comstock, Martha mustered a crew of experienced women also willing to take the gamble and made her way to Panamint, arriving in the wide-open boom camp in about November 1874. While being an early pioneer of the camp wouldn't ensure her a place in its future society once reform set in, it would offer the advantage of cashing in on the first rush.

That winter, the *Anaheim Gazette* reported that there were "700 men, 10 women and six inches of snow in Panamint and lively times are expected." In Panamint, as in Virginia, there would be competition. The formidable Lola Travis had been on the ground since early September, even before there was a passable road into the camp. Lola was no Julia Bulette, entertaining girlfriends to tea in her parlor. However, she was likely to have been shrewd enough to respect the benefits of solidarity among the inhabitants of Little Chief Street, an alleyway destined to become the camp's red-light district.

Among the town's more ardent promoters was twenty-eight-year-old Jim Bruce, who had come from Missouri by way of Pioche in the early days when, as part of a gang of stagecoach bandits, Panamint seemed as good a place as any to escape the unwanted attentions of the law. But if he had been a bad citizen in Nevada, Bruce appeared to take Panamint seriously. He bought up property in the new camp, sat on the newly established town fire protection board and helped to organize a water company, becoming a solid political player. Amid reports of the scarcity of accommodations in Panamint, when a retired prostitute named Nancy Williams arrived, explaining that she wanted to establish a boardinghouse, Bruce sold her a lot on Main Street for the bargain price of fifty dollars.

Saloons sprang up like weeds, especially along lower Main Street. Two of the more prominent were the Oriental, the first saloon in camp established by Dave Neagle as a board plank balanced over two barrels; and Hays and Phillipay's Panamint Saloon. A dance hall entertainer named Minnie Wells set up shop on Little Chief Street behind the Panamint Saloon in November. By the time a prospector named Edmund Lueba showed up in December, the only restaurant in town remained open all night long, while "there is a coming and going of drunkards, gamblers and women who come to eat and generally make an uproar," he recalled. Leuba would not be able to sleep there, the proprietor said, because "there is no protection from their coarse jests."

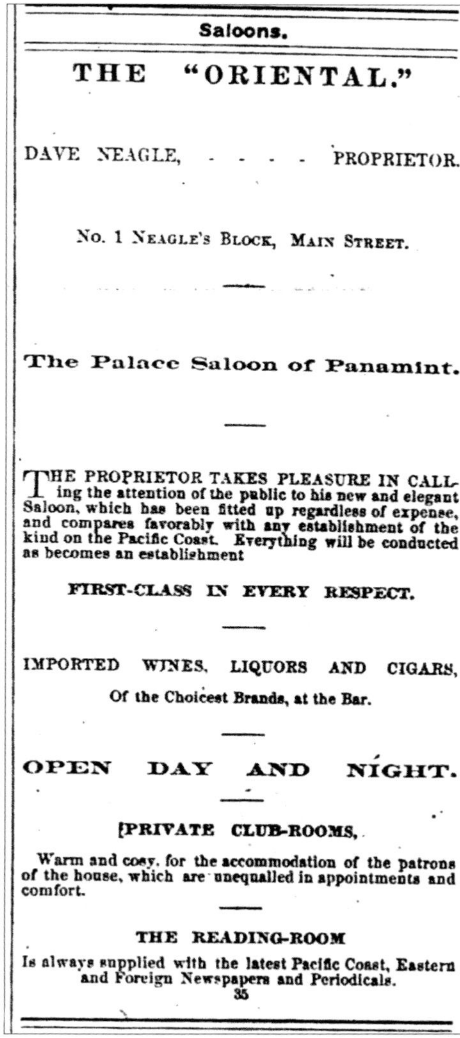

An advertisement for Dave Neagle's Oriental Saloon in 1875. Martha Camp's Panamint brothel was located behind the Oriental. *Courtesy of* Panamint News.

Most likely, Martha had communicated with former Virginia City residents who arrived in the new camp before her and had carefully scoped out the terrain. She purchased a lot on Little Chief Street, connected at the rear with Dave Neagle's saloon. The Oriental was now the most elegant concern in town, complete with a massive billiard table hauled up the canyon at considerable energy and expense.

Little Chief Street soon became a lively part of the camp and was informally rechristened Maiden Lane. It was located at the lower end, while

A study of Irish women who, like Martha Camp, immigrated to the United States during the era of Ireland's Great Hunger indicates that only a small percentage of them chose prostitution as an occupation. The overwhelming majority sought domestic service jobs, like young Delia Donoghue, another Irish woman about Martha's age. Delia had apparently learned to cook and serve as a domestic in the employ of a New York City family and then launched herself in the restaurant business out West. She arrived in Panamint around the same time as Martha Camp and set up the Wyoming (named after a prosperous mine in the district) restaurant "uptown," on the north side of Main Street. She served meals at all hours for seventy-five cents a plate.

While Delia is often portrayed as a "prunella" and a nemesis of sorts to Martha Camp in Panamint City, there is some indication that, while toeing the line of respectability, she did manage to let her hair down in the Wild West. In July 1875, after a camp-wide Independence Day celebration in Panamint the night before, Delia married Joseph Hays, proprietor of the Panamint Saloon where Minnie Wells had lately occupied the ground at the back door. The Panamint Saloon was, in fact, so close to Martha Camp's brothel that Hays was called as a witness to the shooting of Ed Barstow because he could hear the conversation that took place between the men that night from his own room.

After the fall of Panamint, Delia and Joseph Hays moved on, and by 1880, Delia was a widow, operating a restaurant on South C Street in Virginia City. Reformers had by then been successful in cleaning up the Comstock's old Barbary Coast, and Delia's establishment, as respectable as the Wyoming in Panamint, was situated only a few doors down from the house where Martha Camp had lived with Mercedes Navarro a decade before.

businesses catering to the daytime trade were established at the top of the canyon near the mines. There were plenty of saloons, all up and down Main Street. Now there were rooming houses and restaurants as well, including the Wyoming run by a spinster named Delia Donoghue on the upper end of town. Supplies were scarce and expensive, but the camp already boasted doctors and lawyers and all the basic conveniences.

Martha soon befriended Jim Bruce, by then a prominent mover and shaker in Panamint, and the bad-tempered Bruce became Martha's favorite client, the one who was allowed to stay after everyone else had gone home. By the following spring, the camp had weathered a hard winter, its labor force often taking solace on Maiden Lane, and was in the process of becoming a town. It now had a newspaper, a small tri-weekly called the *Panamint News* whose editor, T.S. Harris, had rolled in on the stage not long after Martha. Because the camp had also established a certain reputation for lawlessness, Harris employed a young man named Ed Barstow to guard the newspaper office at night.

On the night of March 22, 1875, Barstow, apparently neglecting his duties at the *Panamint News*, stopped in at Martha's for drinks and fell into boisterous conversation with Jim Bruce and a few other men. Barstow and his friends finally left in the early morning hours, and Bruce stayed behind, intending to spend the night with Martha. The following is her testimony of what happened next:

> *There were some gentlemen at my house on the evening of night of the* 22^{d} *day of March and morning of the* 23^{d}. *They all retired excepting Mr. Bruce, Mr. McAllister and* [Mr. Barstow]. *Barstow left afterward in company with McAllister, and then returned alone.*
>
> *He asked me to open the door. I replied that I was in bed. He said: "If you don't open the door, I will kick it in."*
>
> *I requested him not to do so. He said: "I want to see Jim." I then opened the door. He had a six-shooter in his hand, and remarked: "I've got the long legged s—n of a b—h at last."*
>
> *I endeavored to keep him from entering my bedroom and held on to him and screamed. He got over toward the bureau and put the light out, then the shooting commenced. I don't know who fired the first shot. I saw a flash from Barstow's pistol, and to the best of my belief I think he fired it. He was standing near the bureau when he fired.*
>
> *I did not see Bruce at this time. When I got up and opened the door I left him in bed, and did not see him until he told me to light the lamp. I don't know who shot Barstow.*

> *There were no other persons in the house at the time, to my knowledge, except Miss Sophie Glennen and Mr. Bruce. The doors were open and there might have been. I saw nobody around during the shooting except Bruce and the deceased. The shooting occurred between 2 and 3 A.M.*

Barstow, mortally wounded, was taken to Jim Bruce's home nearby, where, sobering up, he exonerated Bruce of any responsibility and asked that no charges be pressed against him. The shooting was lamented by the *Panamint News*, but editor Harris, understanding the political makeup of the town, didn't press the matter. A coroner's jury exonerated Bruce, and business resumed as usual.

But Panamint, by then, was on the skids. Its mines failed to keep their surface promise, and all eyes turned to Darwin, a new camp on the other side of the Panamint mountain range. Jim Bruce and Dave Neagle made a scouting trip to the new camp and brought back a favorable report, and T.S. Harris began thinking seriously about relocating his newspaper.

In April, Bruce again lost his temper in a gunfight on Main Street in broad daylight. Again he killed his opponent but also suffered serious injuries himself. He was eventually transported to San Francisco for treatment, and by the time he returned to his city of dreams, there was little left to celebrate. At the Oriental, Dave Neagle hung on, hoping the camp would revive, even while most of its residents were swarming to Darwin.

Martha apparently followed Neagle's lead and held out in Panamint until the summer and the town's last hurrah, a Fourth of July celebration during which one of her corsets was reportedly hoisted up a prominent flagpole. But by then the revelry was equally divided between the respectable dance Delia Donoghue organized at the Wyoming, with an unprecedented sixteen ladies in attendance, and the bash Martha threw at her place on Maiden Lane.

Disgusted, Martha mustered her troops and took her place among the wave of immigrants to Darwin. The Panamint gamble had not, perhaps, turned out as she hoped, but Darwin, in a more reasonable and accessible location, promised better things. No record survives of how long she might have remained in that camp, and there is some indication that she may have moved on to Pioche. But if she stayed any length of time, she would have been on hand when Nancy Williams, a retired prostitute turned boardinghouse keeper who had also migrated from Panamint, was murdered under circumstances eerily similar to those surrounding the death of Julia Bulette.

EPILOGUE

Though Darwin limped along after the first flush of its boom was over, it remained a rough and violent camp. Probably around 1879, Martha took her cue from several other Virginia City veterans and eventually headed for the town of Bodie, California. The Bodie economy had been struggling along for years but was then experiencing a new boom cycle. Its Bonanza Avenue was the heart of the Bodie tenderloin, and Martha opened a brothel there.

Bodie's Bonanza Avenue was on par with Virginia City's South C Street of old when it came to violence and mayhem, with regular shootings and fisticuffs. In the fifteen years prior to her time in Bodie, Martha had always been a witness or a victim, rather than a participant, in the violence occurring all around her. However, in 1880, nearing the age of forty, her temper finally snapped. An article in the *Bodie Daily Standard* reported that she chased an unruly customer out of her brothel and down the street, firing five shots at him as she went.

After that, she apparently gave up on following the boom camp circuit and went instead to San Francisco, where in 1885 she accused another man of threatening her life and smashing out the windows of her brothel.

From there she moved on to Oakland, where a *Tribune* reporter wrote of her in 1888: "Madame Camp is one of the regulars of the lower Franklin Street squad and is supposed to be hardened to the core." In May, she made headlines when she refused to return one of her lodgers' trunks until the bill was paid for laundry, board and the wages of a Chinese manservant.

In June, she made headlines again, not in connection with more mayhem but for being unwilling to accept into her brothel a seventeen-year-old girl whose boyfriend was pushing her to become a prostitute. "I am not yet so steeped in sin that I want to see others sin to my level," she said in court when the young man was brought up on felony charges for placing a minor in a house of prostitution. "There are altogether too many of us in the sinful business now."

And perhaps Madam Camp retired soon after, as the Oakland police began a series of raids on Franklin Street designed to close down the brothels and drive the prostitutes out of town. Or at least to round them up in their nightgowns and leave them standing on a street corner waiting for the paddy wagon. Martha was caught up in such a raid toward the end of the year, forfeited a twenty-dollar bond and subsequently disappeared from the historical record.

Notorious

In her brief but colorful tenure in the annals of the mining camp tenderloins, Martha Camp crossed paths with more famous figures and hovered at the edges of more notorious events than any other woman of her time in Death Valley. Her friendship with the now legendary Julia Bulette thrust her briefly into the limelight, and during that time, she may also have met or even been friends with Mark Twain. Twain mentions her, though not by name, in his account of the hanging of John Millain (an event they probably both attended) for the *Chicago Republican*. He may also have been a friend of her deceased husband, H.B. Camp.

Several of Martha's Panamint associates also went on to be involved in other notorious events in the history of the Old West. After Panamint, her former lover Jim Bruce moved on to Deadwood, in what was then the Dakota Territories. He was considered one of the pioneers of that infamous camp where Wild Bill Hickok was gunned down in 1876 and Calamity Jane drank and fought in its saloons for many years to come. While in Deadwood, Bruce engaged in several more gunfights but was best known for beating up his girlfriend, dance hall entertainer Lena Waters, in 1883. Bruce finally married and settled down in Columbia, Nevada, near Goldfield, where he spent the rest of his life operating a saloon and restaurant.

Minnie Wells (who operated out of the back door of the Panamint Saloon) also went on to perform on stage at Deadwood's Gem Theater as a "serio-comic vocalist." Later, a Mrs. Dr. Minnie Wells set up practice in Los Angeles, where she was twice convicted of practicing medicine without a license. Dr. Wells specialized in female ailments.

Dave Neagle, Martha's landlord at the Oriental in Panamint, moved on to Tombstone, Arizona, where he succeeded Virgil Earp (who later moved on to Goldfield, where he died of pneumonia) as chief of police after the gunfight at the O.K. Corral. Eventually he became a U.S. marshal and was involved in a shooting that set a precedent for the use of deadly force by the U.S. Marshal Service. Many disappointed Panaminters followed Neagle's example and sought their fortunes in Tombstone, but there is no indication that Martha was ever among their number.

Senator William Stewart, who had backed Panamint with the full force of his fortune and reputation, suffered considerable losses in the venture. But he was still in the mining business by the time the new Nevada boom began thirty years later and soon relocated to the promising camp of Rhyolite, Nevada.

T.S. Harris, the intrepid editor who published the *Panamint News* and chronicled the gunfight in Martha's bedroom, moved on to Darwin, where he published the *Coso Mining News*; then to Bodie, where he published the *Bodie Evening Standard*; and finally to Los Angeles. In later years, he was sent to prison for murder and eventually committed suicide upon his release.

Chapter 4

A TALE OF TWO FEATHERLEGS

By 1877, the camp of Darwin was two years old and at its zenith. Some two thousand inhabitants kept it in perpetual motion, hustling around the clock to move the ore shipments out of the surrounding mines. Resourceful restaurateurs served food all night long, and the twenty-six saloons did a lively business in the hours between sunup and sundown. At 4:00 a.m. on the morning of September 12, when a stocky young gambler named Jack McGinnis set out to visit a friend of his, he was one of many moving about the town streets.

Nancy Williams was an "old fairy" who kept a boardinghouse on the lower end of Darwin's Main Street. At forty-five or fifty, she was considered old by mining camp standards. Where she'd spent the early days of her life nobody knew and, in keeping with mining camp etiquette, nobody asked. But by the time she reached Darwin, she was well known and well liked, having been on the parlor house circuit through the glory days of Idaho, Montana and Nevada. Like most other Darwinites, she'd tried her hand at Panamint and come down from there when the camp was still young. In the Death Valley boom camps, they called her Aunt Nancy, but those who remembered—or had heard the stories of earlier days, before she married James Williams in Blackfoot City—called her Featherlegs.

Williams's house, a twenty-five- by thirty-foot frame building next door to the Headquarters Saloon, was dark when McGinnis got there and let himself in, lighting a match. In the feeble light, he saw the place in disarray—a trunk flung open, Williams's hat lying out on her bed, but no sign of the woman.

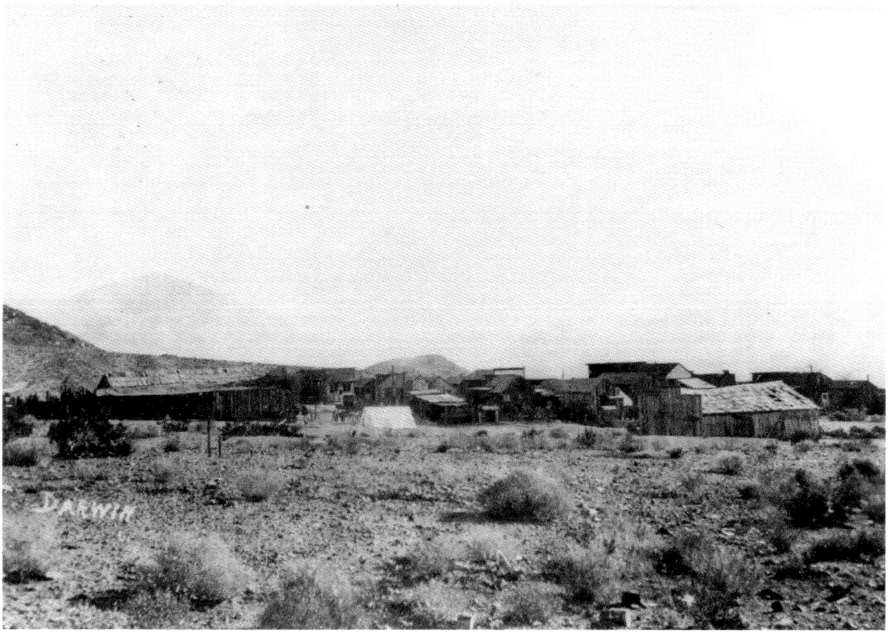

Darwin's Main Street, circa 1870s. *Courtesy of Death Valley National Park Archives.*

The match burned down, and McGinnis went next door to borrow more from several Mexicans who were gambling there.

The next match he struck revealed Williams lying facedown on the floor, where McGinnis figured she'd fallen in a drunken stupor. But looking closer, he saw blood on her face.

McGinnis fled to the Darwin Chop House nearly two blocks away. There he convinced Isaac Giles, who was taking a lunch break from his Corner Saloon, to return with him and verify that Williams was dead. That done, the two went in search of Constable William Welch, a shopkeeper who, in his alter identity as Darwin's night watchman, was often lauded in the local newspaper as the "guardian angel of the town." Welch searched the house for clues and found none but noticed two oyster cans containing nearly $600 worth of receipts, money orders, local mining company scrip and silver bullion. This amounted to a small fortune in carefully saved assets but nothing a burglar could easily spend in camp.

It was widely believed, in the way of boom camps where rumors flourished, that Williams hid large sums of money around her house. Unlike many boom camp followers, who lived close to the edge and often died ill and penniless, Williams had been tending to her future. She owned her home and the lot

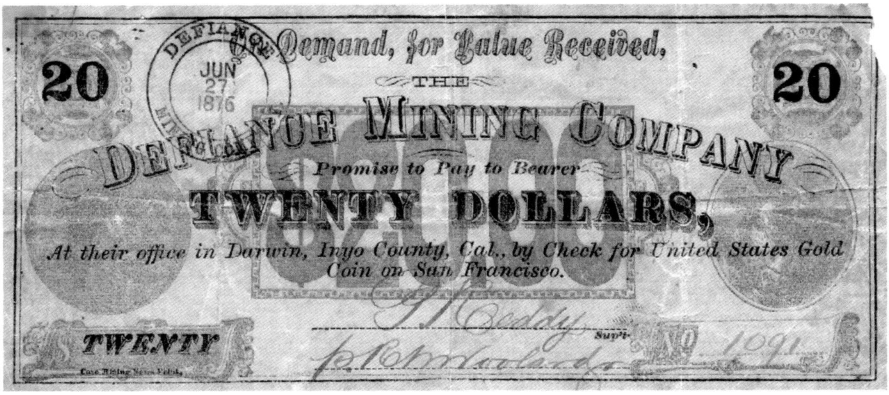

Defiance Company mining scrip, like the kind found in Nancy Williams's house after she was murdered. *Courtesy of Eastern California Museum.*

it sat upon in Darwin outright and regularly deposited her lodging house income, through the local Wells Fargo office, into an account at the Masonic Bank in San Francisco.

But that future she saved for so carefully was canceled out by an unknown assailant who, according to the local coroner, whacked Williams three times on the left side of her head with something like the butt end of a revolver while she held up her hands to defend herself. Then, when she fell to the ground, he hit her one last time, cracking the back of her skull. And that was how McGinnis found her.

The next day, several of Williams's friends, both men and women, gathered to lament her fate, dress the body and prepare her as best they could for her final journey. They walked with her in procession to the graveyard, perhaps with Lola Travis and Martha Camp (who couldn't help but have been reminded of her friend Julia Bulette) among their number. Cerro Gordo saloonkeeper Mary Morales arrived on the stage in time for the funeral. Together they buried Aunt Nancy and eulogized her as a selfless, kindhearted woman known for "alleviating distress by her means whenever an opportunity offered, and giving from her purse to all public enterprises."

Emotions ran high, and Williams's friends and admirers, and others who just wanted to see justice done, pledged vengeance for her death in the form of a collective reward of over $1,200 for the capture of whoever had committed this deed. Sheriff Thomas Passmore alone pledged $250 on behalf of his office and $50 as a private citizen. All of the men who had been present that night and seen Williams lying on the floor with her head smashed in—all of them, oddly enough, except Jack McGinnis—signed

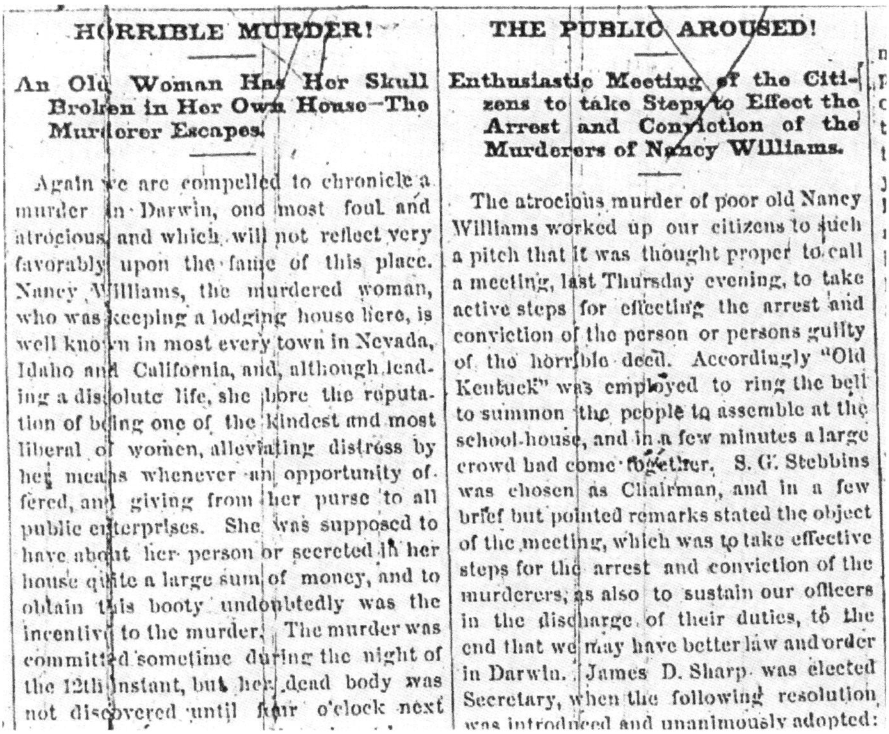

HORRIBLE MURDER!

An Old Woman Has Her Skull Broken in Her Own House—The Murderer Escapes.

Again we are compelled to chronicle a murder in Darwin, one most foul and atrocious, and which will not reflect very favorably upon the fame of this place. Nancy Williams, the murdered woman, who was keeping a lodging house here, is well known in most every town in Nevada, Idaho and California, and, although leading a dissolute life, she bore the reputation of being one of the kindest and most liberal of women, alleviating distress by her means whenever an opportunity offered, and giving from her purse to all public enterprises. She was supposed to have about her person or secreted in her house quite a large sum of money, and to obtain this booty undoubtedly was the incentive to the murder. The murder was committed sometime during the night of the 12th instant, but her dead body was not discovered until four o'clock next

THE PUBLIC AROUSED!

Enthusiastic Meeting of the Citizens to take Steps to Effect the Arrest and Conviction of the Murderers of Nancy Williams.

The atrocious murder of poor old Nancy Williams worked up our citizens to such a pitch that it was thought proper to call a meeting, last Thursday evening, to take active steps for effecting the arrest and conviction of the person or persons guilty of the horrible deed. Accordingly "Old Kentuck" was employed to ring the bell to summon the people to assemble at the school-house, and in a few minutes a large crowd had come together. S. G. Stebbins was chosen as Chairman, and in a few brief but pointed remarks stated the object of the meeting, which was to take effective steps for the arrest and conviction of the murderers, as also to sustain our officers in the discharge of their duties, to the end that we may have better law and order in Darwin. James D. Sharp was elected Secretary, when the following resolution was introduced and unanimously adopted:

Coso Mining News, September 15, 1877.

their names to the pledge sheet. Subscription forms to collect even more pledges were circulated throughout the nearby camps.

In the end, however, it all came to naught. The gambling Mexicans were questioned and released. No solid evidence surfaced. The coroner's jury returned a verdict of murder by person or persons unknown. Sheriff Passmore continued to follow leads on the case for several months, even traveling away from Darwin in his efforts, but never landed the culprit.

When no family came forward to claim Williams's property, it reverted to the county, and the following spring, her personal effects were sold at auction. Her lodging house and the small kitchen behind it were maintained by her estate, under the supervision of a county executor, until the fall of 1880, when they were sold for $50 to C.F. O'Brion, who owned a general store across the street. O'Brion thought highly of Aunt Nancy and was among those who pledged money for the capture of her killer.

Eventually, with a labor war looming on the horizon and an unabated crime spree in full swing in Darwin, Passmore gave up on the case. Before long, Passmore himself was killed in a shootout, and the murder of Nancy Williams remained unsolved.

That was the official version, the one that stood unquestioned for nearly seventy years. But it isn't the only version of the story.

Sometime after the murder of Nancy Williams, a young man named Oliver Roberts, acting as substitute constable in the nearby camp of Lookout, was called upon to break up a deadly brawl between Jack McGinnis, who was one of the principal witnesses in the Williams investigation, and another man named Peter Kelly. Roberts figured he knew what the trouble was since Kelly, a hard drinker with a loose tongue, had recently confided that he knew a terrible secret about McGinnis.

Oliver Roberts de la Fontaine had come of age in the chaotic milieu of Darwin's early days and was an old man of twenty by the time Williams died in 1877. That year, he made his own contribution to the local body count, firing in self-defense at a known bad man. He worked as a security guard, stagecoach driver and Wells Fargo messenger; tried his hand at prospecting; and often substituted as acting constable in Lookout, where he briefly ran a saloon. Or at least those were the claims he made in his memoirs.

Roberts also claimed he was on hand the night Williams died, but his account of the event is wildly different than the version appearing in newspapers of the day. Roberts's details were at odds in almost every particular—from the murder weapon to the amount of blood on the scene to who found the body to what kind and how much money was in Williams's house to when she was buried. His tale, contradicting published sworn testimony by at least two respected men, is questionable, and in fact, when Roberts's memoirs were finally published in 1931, the editor omitted the story entirely.

But while he may not have actually been on the scene that night, Roberts was familiar with the case—familiar enough to believe that it was Jack McGinnis who killed Nancy Williams.

It wouldn't be the first time McGinnis had taken a life under questionable circumstances. Five months earlier, one of his former business partners was found shot dead in the street late at night. Less than an hour later, the sheriff found McGinnis, indicated by a variety of witnesses as the prime suspect, at home in bed as if nothing untoward had occurred. McGinnis claimed self-defense and, at the time of the Williams murder, had yet to stand trial for the shooting.

Roberts's version of what happened the night of September 12 begins with the same principal character, Jack McGinnis, who arrived at the home of Nancy Williams in the early morning hours. But Roberts contended that McGinnis found her alive and demanded that she give him money. "McGinnis was a bad man though he did not look it," Roberts wrote. "He would get wild to gamble and in desperation to carry out that desire would do anything. This is why he killed Featherlegs."

When she could not produce anything other than company scrip, bank orders and silver bullion no longer being accepted as currency in town, McGinnis lost his temper and beat her to death. Then he left and returned later, pretended to discover the body and went for help. He gave his sworn testimony and was, at least officially, never under suspicion of any kind. McGinnis walked away from the Williams murder, Roberts said, but it would plague his conscience. That's why he went after Peter Kelly, the only near witness to his crime.

Kelly told Roberts he had seen McGinnis in the hall of Williams's house at about one thirty on the night of the murder and that McGinnis told him, "If you ever tell anyone you saw me here I will kill you too. Now get out!"

While McGinnis had a fair chance of escaping punishment for the shooting of his business partner, the murder of Featherlegs was different. "In those days men fought and killed men, and easily ran free of the law, but woe unto one who harmed a woman," Roberts wrote twenty years later when he sat down to record his memoirs.

After Roberts broke up the fight between McGinnis and Kelly, he begged Kelly to tell what he had seen, but Kelly, badly beaten and fearful for his life, refused. Roberts went to the sheriff, who "advised me to keep it quiet and said that they would work up the case and land someone in jail."

Again, nothing came of it. Within a year, Roberts claimed, he himself was involved in a gunfight with McGinnis and seriously wounded him. But again Roberts is contradicted by a contemporary newspaper account, which states that McGinnis was killed in Lookout during a shootout with a man named Frank Fitzgerald.

According to Roberts, he had done his best to reveal McGinnis as the murderer, and perhaps to collect the associated reward, but in this he was unsuccessful. So his version of the story remained untold at the time and untold fifty years later when his memoir was published as the book *The Great Understander* and didn't see the light of day until it was included in a serial of the original manuscript in the *Pony Express Courier* of 1953.

It seemed that the puzzle was solved at last, but Roberts's unreliable description of the night of the murder, as well as his false claims to have participated in other incidents of the time, leave plenty of room for doubt.

Perhaps there is one other possible solution to this crime, now over a century and a quarter old.

About a year and a half after Williams's death, one thousand miles away in the wilds of Wyoming, a lonely ranch wife named Mrs. Demmon saddled up her horse and prepared to ride over to the home of her nearest neighbor. The neighbor ran a disreputable roadhouse on the Cheyenne–Black Hills trail, but she was a woman in men's country, and Mrs. Demmon was starved for company. Unfortunately, the only company she would find when she arrived was the dead body of her middle-aged friend, known as Madam Featherlegs.

Featherlegs had been dead two or three days, shot in the gut while filling up her water bucket at a nearby spring. Tracks around her corpse looked like those made by her live-in lover, a shady character known as Dangerous Dick Davis. Any valuables she might have had were gone from her rough cabin. Mrs. Demmon summoned the authorities, and they buried old Featherlegs on the spot with little fanfare. No one knew where she had come from or even her real name.

Until a few years later, when Dangerous Dick Davis surfaced again in Louisiana, on trial for murder and robbery. Before he was hanged for that crime, he finally revealed the story of Wyoming's Madam Featherlegs. Her real name, he said, was Charlotte Shepard, and she had been part of a gang of ex-Confederate marauders prowling the Louisiana swamps after the Civil War. One by one, the members of the gang had been hunted down and eliminated, including Shepard's sons, who had died in a vigilante hanging. Shepard and Davis, the only two survivors, fled Louisiana and took refuge in the wide-open West. But despite their isolation in the wilds of Wyoming, they hadn't gone far enough, and eventually, Charlotte's fate caught up with her.

There is no evidence to link the murder of Charlotte Shepard to the murder of Nancy Williams—just a long list of coincidences tying their stories together across distance and time. Two women, both middle aged, both former prostitutes running disreputable rooming houses in remote western locations, both using the alias Featherlegs, both murdered within a year and a half of each other—one for no apparent reason. Could Nancy Williams have been mistakenly murdered by someone seeking vengeance on Charlotte Shepard?

Most likely we'll never know the answer to that question, but it turns out that even in death, Williams's and Shepard's stories followed parallel lines. While many of Nancy Williams's friends and neighbors grieved over her grave and pledged to see justice done, they were perhaps thinking more of protecting the living than honoring the dead. For when the funeral was over, the grave was left unmarked and untended.

And so it remained until 1880, when C.F. O'Brion, the storekeeper who had lived across the street from Williams and bought her house at auction, lamented in a letter to the editor of the *Inyo Independent* that the grave had "not one solitary strip of board" on it. Coroner A.J. Lank, administrator of Williams's estate, soon set the situation to rights by ordering a small fence and headstone. At some point, probably around the same time, a large granite obelisk was erected over Nancy Williams's grave. It still stands there today, the most imposing marker in the old cemetery, though slightly pockmarked where an anonymous rifleman used it for target practice.

In 1864, a madam called Moll Featherlegs brought charges against a mean drunk named J.A. Slade, who invaded and vandalized her brothel in Virginia City, Montana. Before she could collect any damages from him, Slade was arrested by the Citizen's Vigilance Committee and hanged for a variety of other crimes in what is today a much-debated act of frontier justice. Among the members of the committee was one Captain James Williams. Although this James Williams went on to marry a woman named Elizabeth and have many children, Darwin's Nancy Featherlegs also married a man named James Williams in Montana and could very well have been Montana's Moll Featherlegs.

Shepard's lonely grave was left undisturbed for about fourteen years, until the day two young boys decided to dig her up for fun. Her body had been slightly mummified, her flaming red hair still intact, said one of the boys many years later, and the sight of her scared them so badly that they immediately dropped the coffin back into place and ran for their lives.

Sometime in the late 1940s or early 1950s, a couple from Los Angeles visited Darwin and lifted Williams's gravestone to take home as a souvenir. But before they had gotten far from town, a series of mishaps convinced them the stone was cursed, and they mailed it back to Darwin, begging that it be replaced on the grave.

In 1964, as part of the hoopla generated by a reenactment of the Denver-to-Deadwood stage run, local promoters placed a 3,500-pound pink granite

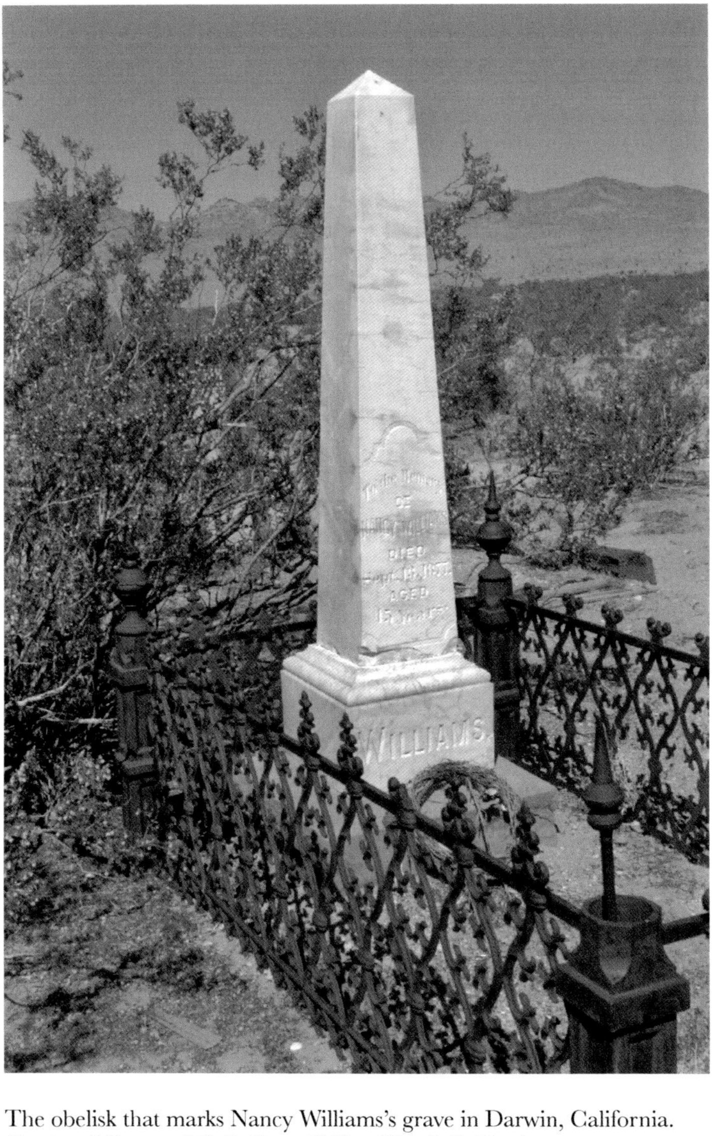

The obelisk that marks Nancy Williams's grave in Darwin, California. *Courtesy of Roger and Cecile Vargo, Explore Historic California.*

monument over Charlotte Shepard's grave and dedicated it with what was likely to be more pomp and ceremony than the woman had ever known in her lifetime. It is touted today as the only monument to a prostitute in the United States.

So while the two Featherlegs haven't exactly been resting in peace all this while, perhaps they might take some measure of comfort in the knowledge that they certainly have not been forgotten.

Chapter 5

DAUGHTERS OF THE SUN

CHINESE WOMEN IN DARWIN

In November 1875, the stagecoach from Caliente, Nevada, arrived in Darwin and discharged its passengers—several Chinese men and women who had come with baggage in hand to try their luck in the flourishing new camp. The "almond eyed, pig-tailed Celestials," reported Darwin's fledgling *Coso Mining News*, "were received with humorous remarks by numerous friends and admiring Christians."

At the height of anti-Chinese frenzy in America, these remarks, whatever they were, were unlikely to have seemed particularly humorous or admiring to their recipients. Misconceptions about the Chinese were rampant among Anglo Americans, and a prevailing fear of the unknown made bridging the gap between the two cultures almost impossible. Uppermost on the list of stereotypes was the lewd, immoral character of all Chinese women—the "female scum of the Flowery Kingdom," as editor Harris referred to them in the *Panamint News*.

Nearly all Chinese woman arriving in mining camps were assumed to be prostitutes. When reporting the stagecoach arrivals in his newspaper, Harris listed white men traveling with women by the name of the man "and wife," but Chinese men were listed by the name of the man "and woman"—white women were automatically given the benefit of the doubt, while Chinese women were automatically suspect. In truth, there was some basis for this assumption, since very few Chinese women did immigrate in these years for the purpose of joining husbands in America. Of the thousands who were shipped into San Francisco between 1850 and 1880, a large percentage were indentured slaves intended for sale in Chinatown brothels all over the West.

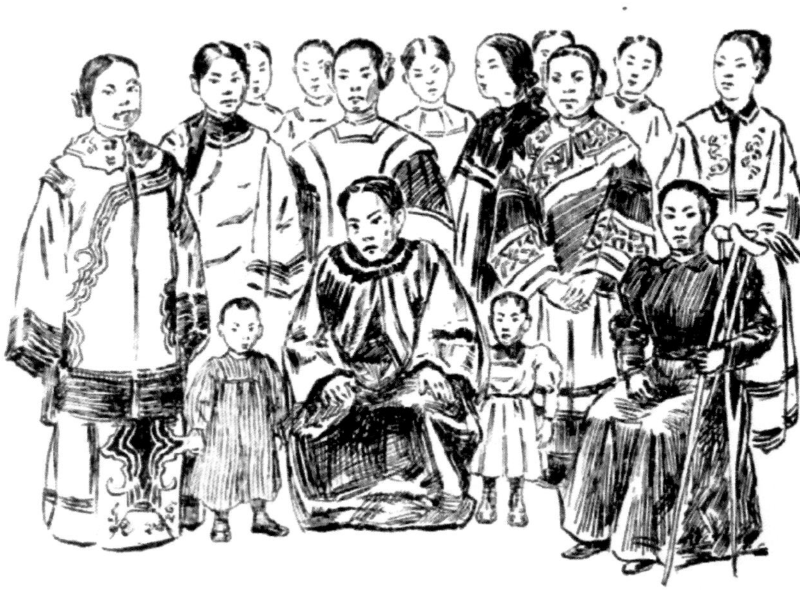

Group of Rescued Slaves at the Methodist Mission.

Former Chinese slave women at a rescue mission in San Francisco. *Courtesy of* San Francisco Chronicle.

Earlier in 1875, Harris had lauded the decision of the U.S. Congress to enact a bill regulating the immigration of Chinese women. The 1875 Page Law was designed to stem the tide of these women being imported, usually against their will, for the purposes of prostitution. It had little effect, however, since its main provision for enforcement was that the captain in charge of each ship should refuse to carry such "obnoxious" persons. The influx of indentured Chinese women continued.

By the spring of 1876, the *Coso Mining News* was following a Senate inquiry into the traffic in Chinese slave prostitutes coming through San Francisco. While public outcry railed against the traffic in these women, contemporary newspaper articles rarely portrayed them with any compassion. The protests were not made on behalf of the women themselves or the ill treatment they received but, rather, on behalf of the promising young white men who, it was widely believed, would be ruined by contact with them.

By 1880, Harris and his newspaper were long gone from Darwin, and the ongoing campaign against the Chinese in America had resulted in a whole body of legislation designed to keep them firmly segregated and marginalized from the larger Anglo society. Darwin was then small and struggling, with an official population of eighty-five. The Chinese section, clinging to a hill in a couple of washes at the south end of town, housed about a fourth of the local residents. Most of the people here were men and worked at menial manual labor jobs. But there were also four women living in the neighborhood, one a housewife and the other three listed by the census enumerator that year as prostitutes. In the census records of the mining camps in the Death Valley region, these are the only women ever identified as prostitutes.

Each of those three was old for a Chinese prostitute. The statistics gathered from what data was collected at the time indicate that the work lives of these women usually began in their early teens and might last ten years. The youngest of the three, Ah Chap, was then twenty-eight. Ah My was thirty-two, and Fah Kee, the oldest, was thirty-seven.

But perhaps in the small, isolated town of Darwin, things were somewhat different. Each of the women lived in a separate dwelling, and each lived with a single man (except Ah Chap, who lived with two men). It's hard to imagine, across the lines of culture and time, what these arrangements truly meant to the people involved. Statistics indicate that the women were probably indentured slaves, owned or managed by and working for the men they lived with. But perhaps there is another possibility.

None of these women could read or write in English. It's likely they could not speak it, either. That left the census enumerator to decide for himself what their occupations were. While enumerators were trained to seek objective data, they were as vulnerable to common prejudice as anyone else. One researcher contends that several wives in the 1870 Virginia City census were identified as prostitutes because the enumerator could not understand the culturally foreign concept of second wives.

Is it possible, then, that these Chinese women in Darwin and the men they lived with, two of whom were employed in the prosaic jobs of washmen and the other as a cook, were involved in life partnerships the enumerator failed to recognize or was unwilling to legitimize?

It is possible but, in the end, unlikely. Each one of the women had been born in China. Perhaps they were all from poor families, "big footed peasant girls" who brought a lower price and therefore could be spared to a remote desert mining camp. The hard road ahead for them may have begun at some point in their early teens, when each had been tricked, sold or even pawned by their families into prostitution. Each then made the long ocean voyage to San Francisco, where, if she wasn't already aware of the arrangement she had entered into, she might be surprised to discover that the contract she had signed to become a domestic servant had, in fact, locked her into a life of sexual slavery.

Girls who had been thus indentured were trained in San Francisco, and the work would vary according to the station she had been assigned. More elegant and expensive women might be sold to a single owner and set up much like a mistress. Women of lower stations would be outfitted in simple dark cotton trousers and pajama-style shirts, with gingham kerchiefs tied over their heads to indicate their status and profession, and would be quickly "broken in" and sold. These women were likely to be introduced to opium early on as a means of pacifying and making them easier to manage. While the very few surviving accounts suggest that these women saw it as their duty to perform whatever service was required of them in honor of their families, they were still frequently devastated by being taken from their homelands and thrust into a life where marriage or any kind of family bond was unlikely.

The average Chinese indentured prostitute in an American mining camp was likely to live a life of violence, disease, disrespect, addiction, poverty and cruelty—all in a language and culture she did not understand. She would receive no healthcare, no pay, no time off and little human kindness. But though they would find little protection in America, author Albert Evans observed that Chinese women could find companionship and solidarity among themselves.

"They are mere children in point of intellect," he wrote about the indentured Chinese prostitutes he observed in San Francisco's Chinatown in 1873, although since he could not have conversed with any of them in their native language, he could not have known anything about their intellect. "Having no education whatever, and no experience of the world outside of the narrow alleys in which they have always lived, and the emigrant ship in which they were brought over to this country. They have their likes and their dislikes, of course, and become attached to each other in a childish way, frequently being seen walking together on the streets, hand in hand, like little Caucasian sisters going home from school."

For Ah Chap, Fah Kee and Ah My, their paths led eventually to Darwin, where, as the population trickled away, their status as the only available women in camp may have earned them more care and attention than their sisters in larger cities.

Dr. Wing Wo, a Chinese healer and successful Darwin businessman, had gotten in early on the Darwin boom and set himself up in a comfortable establishment on First Avenue. He advertised that his medicines were made "from roots and herbs gathered in the Chinese kingdom, and use no poisonous substances whatsoever." Wo's ad went on to say that he flattered himself he could "well compete with any Physician in the United States." With Dr. Wo on the scene, if these women were working as prostitutes, perhaps they received treatment for the variety of ailments that was likely to plague them.

In 1876, the *Coso Mining News* reported, "The testimony of a Chinese boy goes to show the fact that three of his countrymen own 1,000 Chinese harlots. He says they are bought in China for about $150, but here they are worth from $800 to $900." Research indicates that this figure was probably exaggerated and that, on average, the purchase price and handling expenses for each prostitute was about $600. If the woman then earned between twenty-five and fifty cents per transaction and saw between five and ten clients per day every day she was not menstruating, she could earn this back in the first year. But she would often never see a penny of the money, and even after all the expenses incurred on her behalf were paid, she was never given any share of her earnings.

After the first year, each indentured woman was a means of pure profit for whoever controlled her. In isolated Darwin, where replacing her would be difficult and costly, perhaps the men were inclined to guard their investments more carefully and provide healthcare and proper nutrition. The work pace was slower here, where the population was small. It's also entirely possible that the men in charge of these women were themselves essentially owned by the Chinese organized crime bosses in San Francisco and were only the keepers of these women.

Inyo Independent

INDEPENDENCE, CAL.
Saturday,........June 1, 1872

Shooting

At Cerro Gordo, on the evening of the 27th ultimo, a couple of Chinamen named respectively Lee Tu Pang and See Kee, got into active hostilities over the possession of a moon eyed daughter of the sun, resulting in the severe wounding and probable death of one of them. It appears that Pang owned the woman, who left him and went to the protection of Kee, renouncing her former master. Pang, in an effort to recover his prize, goes after Kee with a pistol, which he discharged once and received in return a shot in the leg above the knee, sustaining a bad compound fracture. Other Chinamen refused to allow amputation, and the probabilities are that his death will result. See Kee was arrested and examined before Justice Fox and discharged, on evidence as stated.

This scenario begs the question did these men and women, living so closely together, ever fall in love or try to marry? Research indicates that if they did, they were dealt swift vengeance by the controlling tong. In some cases, however, men who fell in love with indentured slave prostitutes were able to purchase their lover's freedom and offer marriage and a home.

Editor Harris, in spite of his own snide remarks about Chinese people, may have been more liberal-minded than many of his contemporaries, for he served as witness at a wedding of a Chinese couple in Darwin in 1875. Whether the union of Wong Kehoe and Ling Tong was one that would release the bride from indenture as a prostitute is unknown, but statistics indicate that usually if a man sent for a wife from China, they were married in the traditional Chinese ceremony when she arrived. An American ceremony might not be seen as binding in the Chinese community but could often serve to legally liberate an indentured slave prostitute from her owner.

If statistics and established patterns can be relied upon in guessing at the true circumstances of their lives, Darwin's three Chinese prostitutes were probably all engaged in a trade they wouldn't have chosen on their own and spent their days servicing customers in small dugouts carved into the side of the Lucky Jim wash. They and the thousands of others like them throughout the West had little to look forward to at the end of the day, nor at the end of what was likely to be a short life. In a large city, when the inevitable time came that an indentured Chinese prostitute became too diseased or too old and exhausted to work, she might be released to one of the rescue missions or simply locked in a dark room to die. In a struggling mining camp like Darwin, she might simply be turned out in the street.

In contrast to this harsh picture, however, Benson Tong, in his book *Unsubmissive Women*, suggests that not all Chinese slave prostitutes were passive victims of their fate. His research into the lives of Chinese prostitutes in San Francisco led him to the conclusion that even under these oppressive conditions, many women were able to buy their freedom, change their circumstances for the better or at least embrace the profession thrust upon them with a philosophical acceptance. In the Death Valley camps, a surviving stagecoach log suggests that at least one Chinese woman may have been a free agent. At any rate, she had the freedom to travel alone, arriving unescorted in Cerro Gordo in 1877.

No record exists to show what became of Ah Chap, Ah My or Fah Kee, or of the men they lived with. Whether they remained in Darwin or moved on to find work in some other place is unknown. In the end, the only thing known for sure about these three women is that they all happened to be in this same small town on the day the census enumerator came to call.

Chapter 6

AMARGOSA STREET 1905–1910

THE RISE AND FALL OF RHYOLITE'S RED-LIGHT DISTRICT

In April 1905, not long after the town of Rhyolite, Nevada, was platted and put up for sale, a woman named Mable Vaughn plunked down $150 for a lot on the newly mapped corner of Amargosa Street and Broadway. Vaughn was the first woman to buy property in Rhyolite, and there, on an empty patch of scruffy desert, she would eventually build a sumptuously elegant two-story frame brothel, complete with a wide, shady veranda, and open her doors to the greatest mining metropolis in the West. Big men with big money were arriving in Rhyolite every day, and their construction and mining ventures employed other men by the hundreds. There was money to be made anywhere you looked, and Vaughn intended to earn her share of it.

But while the rush to Rhyolite was on, the building up of the town's red-light district took time to accomplish. For the first year or more of the camp's existence, the new tenderloin was sparsely populated, and Vaughn began by doing business out of a small crib on an otherwise empty lot. In those days, lower Amargosa Street boasted only one substantial structure, the Adobe Dance Hall. Made, as its name implies, of adobe bricks, the dance hall was a large building occupying two lots on the corner of Amargosa and Colorado Streets. Originally built in May 1905, it was owned by an old prospector named Bob Bynum. The Adobe boasted a dance floor and bar where lonely men paid women for the privilege of shuffling them around to live piano music or paid whiskey prices for tea and water drinks for their partners. For those who were more

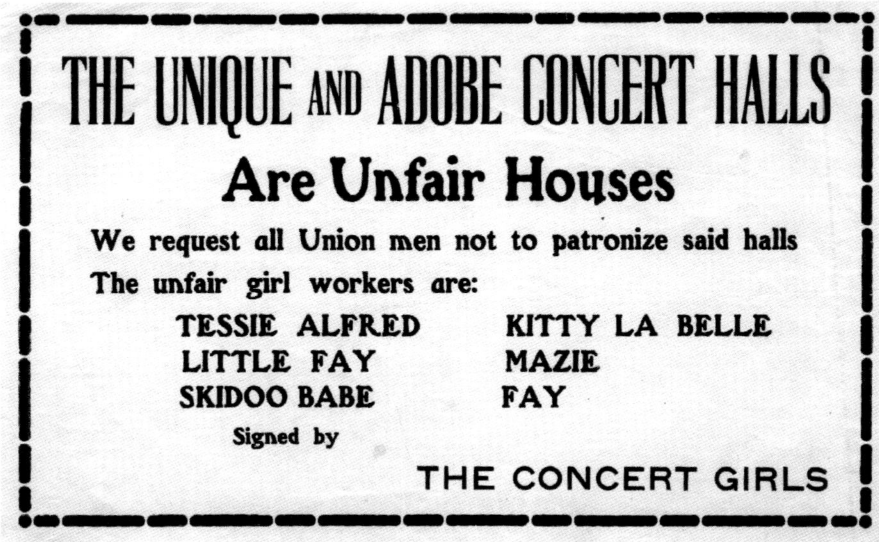

THE UNIQUE AND ADOBE CONCERT HALLS

Are Unfair Houses

We request all Union men not to patronize said halls

The unfair girl workers are:

TESSIE ALFRED KITTY LA BELLE
LITTLE FAY MAZIE
SKIDOO BABE FAY

Signed by

THE CONCERT GIRLS

A handbill posted on one of the utility poles in Rhyolite around 1907. The Adobe was one of the first and longest-lasting dance halls in Rhyolite. *Courtesy of Nevada State Historical Society.*

serious about their recreation, a long corridor ran alongside the dance floor leading to several small rooms where prostitutes accommodated their clientele.

In the early days, the Adobe was the place where all the women who worked elsewhere along Amargosa Street came to socialize, where they spent holidays such as Christmas and New Year's in an effort to feel a sense of community. It was also a social center for prospectors and miners who gathered not only to drink, dance and dally with women but also to watch locally arranged boxing matches and other sporting events.

Today it's unclear whether the placement of the Adobe set the limits for Rhyolite's red-light district. In Nevada, where prostitution was conditionally legal, it's likely the town fathers (actually a set of brothers named Frank and Pete Busch) planned for their tenderloin at the outset. Whether or not they planned it this way, Rhyolite's tenderloin was soon firmly established in the neighborhood surrounding the Adobe. Within two years, the boundaries had become official.

The series of mining booms that began in Death Valley country after the turn of the twentieth century tended to be of a kinder, gentler variety, with fewer gunfights or barroom brawls. But for prostitutes, this by-the-book era was a sterner, stricter time. It became common practice in the early days of

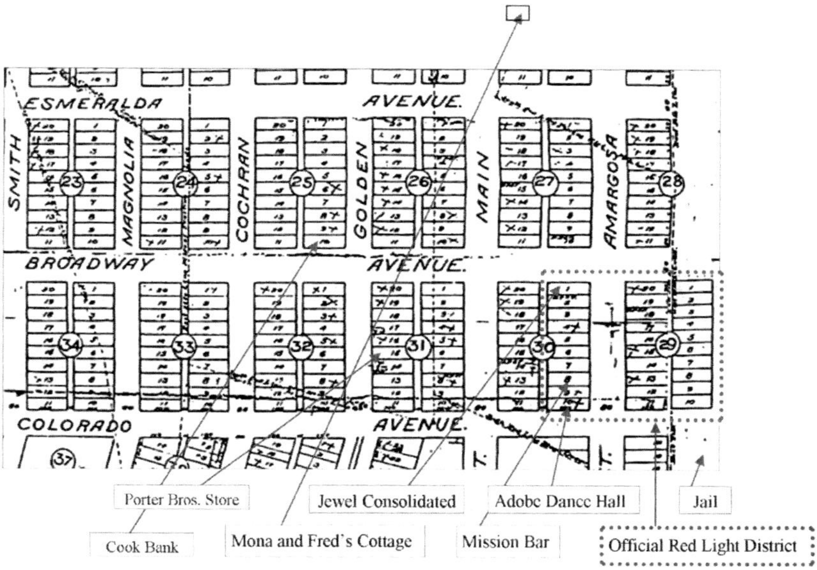

Map of Lower Rhyolite, Nevada
Showing Red Light District, 1908

A map showing the red-light district of the town of Rhyolite. *Courtesy of Nye County Recorder's Office.*

a new camp to draw demarcation lines for the red-light district and devise rules and regulations for its inhabitants. Prostitutes were now carefully, and legally, segregated from the rest of the population.

In Rhyolite, the dance halls, brothels and cribs were confined to a square block-and-a-half area, with Vaughn's brothel marking the northwest outer limits. Officially, the district was bounded on the north by Broadway, on the south by Colorado, on the west by the alley between Main and Amargosa and on the east by Ladd. Thus situated, it was conveniently near the business district only a couple blocks away on Golden Street. A sturdy town jail was eventually constructed on the corner of Colorado and Ladd, marking the tenderloin's southeastern outer limits.

Here, and here only, prostitution was legal and even acceptable as a business endeavor. Unlike California, which had outlawed prostitution entirely, Nevada allowed its counties and towns to govern their own red-light districts with some basic restrictions regarding the placement of schools

Rhyolite Town Ordinance No. 5

Licensing and Regulating Prostitutes

Section No. 1.—Every baudy house and every crib or room within the town limits used and occupied for purposes of prostitution shall be required to have a town license therefor. Such license shall be for one (1) calendar month and the fee therefor shall be five dollars for each inmate for such house, crib or room. The occupation of any such house, crib or room by owner or leaser without first having secured such license shall be deemed an offense and shall be punished as hereinafter provided.

Section No. 2.—No person shall sell or cause to be sold any intoxicating drinks in any house, crib or room within the town limits used or occupied in whole or in part for purposes of prostitution without having first obtained a town license therefor. Such license shall be for one calendar month and the fee therefor shall be twenty-five dollars. Any violation of this section shall be deemed an offense and shall be punished as hereinafter provided.

Section No. 3.—No house, crib or room with the town limits shall be used or occupied as a dance or hurdy gurdy house, or for the purposes of prostitution except within the territory bounded on the north by Broadway, on the south by Colorado street, on the west by the alley between Main and Amargosa streets and on the east by Ladd street of the town of Rhyolite. Any person violating this section shall be deemed guilty of an offense and punished as hereinafter provided.

—Established by Town Board of Rhyolite, August 7, 1907.

and churches in proximity to brothels and dance halls. Within the bounds established by the Rhyolite Board of Trade, the women were free to work at their chosen profession as long as they paid their monthly five-dollar-a-head license fees and did not stray outside the bounds of the established district.

The *Bullfrog Miner*'s Frank Mannix took a philosophical view of the subject when he editorialized that "respectable" residents should not be discouraged by the town board's adoption of an official red-light policy in early 1907: "It

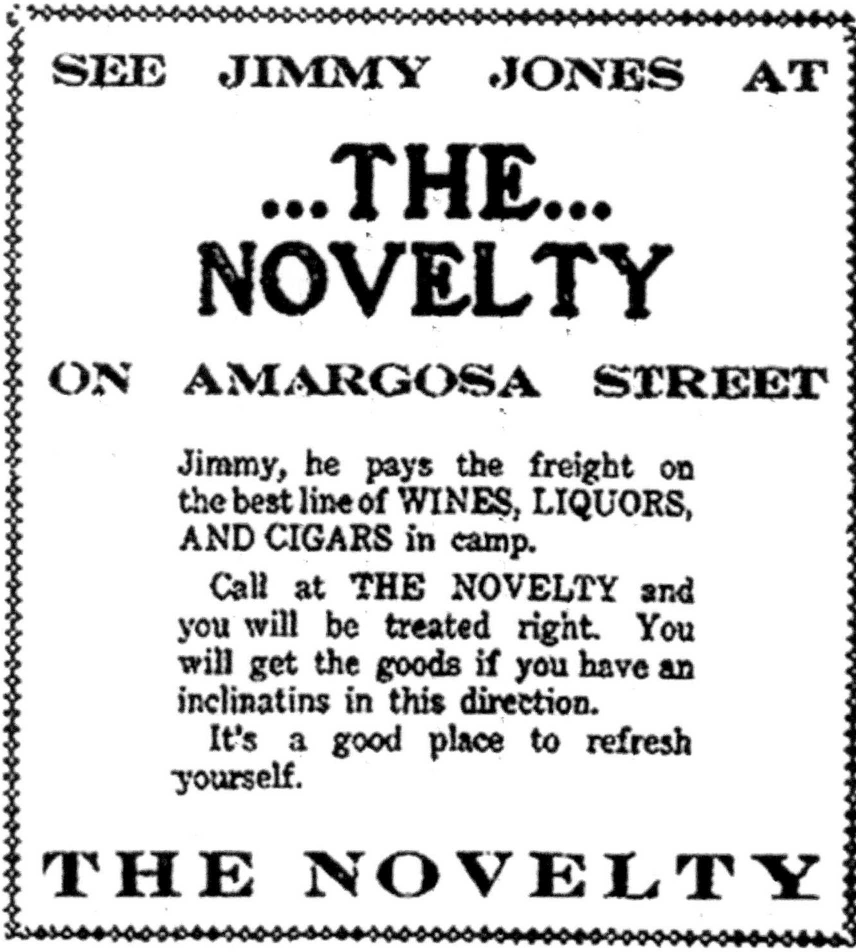

An advertisement for the Novelty Saloon. Few red-light businesses ever advertised in the local newspapers, but Jimmy Jones took the opportunity to support the *Bullfrog Miner*'s 1907 special Christmas edition by placing this item. The Novelty was a frame saloon, complete with a piano, swinging door and rooms off to the side where prostitutes plied their trade. It was located on the east side of Amargosa Street in about the middle of the block. Later, around 1910, the Novelty was apparently relocated across the street and operated by a man named Rainbow Hickman. It was also known as the "Mad House" in those days, and men often left the "respectable" saloons on Main Street, traveled through the alley between and entered the Novelty through the back door. *Courtesy of* Bullfrog Miner.

must not be inferred…that the moral and spiritual life of the community has been neglected. Far from it. With the enforcement of the ordinances the morals of the city will be safeguarded in a practical way and to a practical extent, while much good will accrue in a material sense."

This included not only a substantial tax base but also the money spent on dress goods and furnishings by the women in the upscale houses. Some of these women were so well groomed and elegant that when they stepped out of the red-light district bounds, they were often mistaken for "respectable" ladies. Many of them deposited their earnings at the Bullfrog Bank and Trust on the corner of Main and Broadway, where Mrs. T.M. Gronen often helped out her husband by working as a teller. Later, it would become a family legend that she, an enthusiastic bridge player but rather naïve, frequently tried to recruit these young women for her bridge parties. Mr. Gronen was always grateful when the prostitutes, understanding the difference in their social situations better than the banker's wife, politely declined.

The segregation of prostitutes in Rhyolite didn't apply only to their business practices but reached all levels of social interaction. Prostitutes were discouraged from living or even shopping outside the red-light district, though many of them broke these rules. Mable Vaughn bought a lot in the upscale Eddy's Addition and built a house there, probably used as a residence and a retreat from the demands of the Jewel. But most of the women lived in the brothels and cribs where they worked and spent their leisure as well as their work time inside the restricted district or in saloons and restaurants on the stretch of Main Street that fronted the alleyway connected to the red-light portion of Amargosa Street.

The one place segregation didn't extend, however, was the graveyard. Although some Rhyolite legends claim that prostitutes were denied burial in the local cemetery, surviving information indicates that this is not the case. In one instance, schoolteacher Louise Presser was called upon to comfort a young prostitute on her deathbed and later wrote, "She is one who was buried in the little cemetery on the desert with only a prayer." There was apparently no question of her remains not being accepted for burial.

But outside the somber graveyard, even small children soon learned where the red-light district boundaries were drawn. Nellie Laird lived in Rhyolite as a child and later remembered wanting to befriend another girl whose mother lived in the tenderloin. "She can come to our house anytime she wants," Nellie's mother said, "but you are never, never to go to her house."

Dora Brown remembered being curious about a house under construction across from where she lived with her parents near the railroad depot. The building had "such small rooms with just a door. We would go over there and watch them build until Papa found out what they were for. Just a narrow bed and a chair in them. Mama tried to explain to the older girls what kind of a house it was. Finally, she just told us they were bad places with girls in them. We weren't allowed over there again, nor were we allowed to play on that side of the house."

But it was hard to keep the children away from the red-light district, as the women who worked there not only held the attraction of the unknown and forbidden, but they were also often quite friendly and fun to visit. When Katie Peterson was a little girl in Rhyolite, one of the brothels had a swimming pool. Against her mother's strict prohibition, Katie used to sneak down to the tenderloin, where the women treated her kindly and let her get some relief from the summer heat by taking a dip in their pool.

The "respectable" element in Rhyolite insisted on the strict enforcement of red-light boundaries, and women who refused to "keep their places" could face harsh repercussions. In early January 1907, a delegation from the Miner's Union insisted that the town board be more diligent in its efforts, citing one woman in particular who had broken the rules. The *Bullfrog Miner* reported, "A committee of three was chosen to call upon the proprietress of a certain house of questionable moral repute, which is outside of the 'redlight belt,' and give her notice to vamoose, and if she didn't comply, then the committee was empowered to take such action as necessary in the premises."

But these kinds of infractions were few, and there seemed to be room enough in the designated district to house plenty of brothels, cribs, saloons and dance halls. Vaughn's neighbors varied widely.

Rhyolite's tenderloin was a mixture of the elegant and the sordid. Most of the business done here was conducted at night while the rest of the town slept. In the daylight hours, while Rhyolite's citizens went about the business of building up their town, many of the residents of its red-light district rested behind drawn shades and closed doors. This could be a hard schedule to keep when the desert temperatures climbed in the summer months, but it was a simple fact that bars and brothels rarely prospered in the daytime.

Some of the most valuable businesses in the city were located in this one-block stretch of Amargosa Street, perched alongside tent saloons and narrow frame cribs. Mable Vaughn got a bargain when she bought her corner lot for $150 in 1905. A few months later, lots in the tenderloin were selling for as high as $1,000 apiece. By 1906, the tax assessor valued the Adobe, built with locally made adobe bricks on lots that originally sold for $1 apiece, at $2,200. But the Adobe had been surpassed by then as other businesses on the street hit their stride. Maggie Keely's brothel was valued that same year at $6,490, just a few hundred dollars less than the popular Porter Brothers Store, stocked to the rafters with all kinds of merchandise, a few blocks away.

THE BULLFROG MINER

RHYOLITE, NEV. NOVEMBER 2, 1907

THE DEVIL AMONG THE DRESSMAKERS

A case of more than ordinary importance occupied the attention of Judge Kalahar Thursday afternoon. It was the civil action of Mrs. B.B. Lemmon against Miss Jewel Vaughn, proprietor of the Jewel Consolidated [a brothel on Amargosa Street], for the recovery of $18.95 alleged to be due and owing for work performed on certain kimonos, wrappers and portiers.

The plaintiff stated under oath that the service consisted of remodeling the garments in question and that it had been performed according to blueprint or, clothing it in different words, entirely up to the plans and specifications. The defendant, however, found numerous objections and refused to come through with the cash. The plaintiff was supported by a couple of witnesses who seemed to have a general idea of the business. They had seen her put in several shifts on the job and they stated she exercised unusual care to see that the various parts jibed and the dimensions were according to prescribed measurements. The witnesses thought the work had been performed in strict accordance with the league rules for performing such work.

The testimony of the defendant was diametrically opposed to that of the plaintiff. She said it was a bum job and for that reason she refused to blow across with the simoleons. In the instance of the portiers, she stated the headings were uneven, causing the swinging wall to hang asweking, which interpreted means catternlike, or words to this effect. The kimonos and Mother Hubbards, too, had been irremediably botched. The basque and polonaise failed to connect with the northeast gusset of the off arm, thereby reducing the available potential some 29 kilowatts, and causing whole bunches of trouble. More than this, a new face had to be put on the leading ruffle, and the main workings retimbered before the rags were in the proper condition to appear in polite society. The defendant was likewise supported by two witnesses who were thoroughly next to this brand of carpenter work, and they stated it was about the worst they had ever, ever seen.

The plaintiff was represented by Deputy District Attorney Delaney and the defendant by Judge Horatio Alling. Both attorneys made learned arguments showing an intimate acquaintance with all forms of female attire. It was beautiful to hear them going into details and telling how such wearing apparel should be built.

Judgment was in full to plaintiff.

By 1907, the richly furnished Jewel was worth nearly as much, in terms of real property, as the entire workings of the Montgomery Shoshone Mine, one of the biggest producers in Bullfrog history.

But while Vaughn quickly built up her business, her Rhyolite career began in a small, sparse, one-room building known as a crib. Vaughn's crib was probably better appointed than most. A real estate inventory from a crib in the mining camp of Tonopah in 1907 shows the typical furnishings of such an establishment:

3 small rugs
1 iron bed, springs and mattress
1 quilt
2 pillows
2 dressers
1 carpet
1 bowl and pitcher
1 settee
1 rocking chair
1 pair of portieres
1 heating stove
2 red window shades

By the time Mable Vaughn replaced her small crib with the Jewel Consolidated and her establishment became the reigning belle of Amargosa Street, there were also a significant number of cribs lining the lower portion of the street. For most of the women working in these structures, there was no running water, no toilet facilities and no cooking facilities. But entrepreneurs like Happy Days Diminy, a female prospector who set up a sandwich stand on Amargosa Street to finance her trips into the desert hills, provided easy meals at all hours of the day and night. Rhyolite prostitutes also often met up at popular restaurants a block over on Main Street to eat together and tell one another the latest tenderloin news.

The figures below illustrate the rise in value of properties along Amargosa Street as the town grew into a small desert metropolis:

<u>1906 Tax Assessments in Rhyolite</u>
Adobe worth $2,200
Maggie Keely's brothel (across from the Jewel) worth $6,490
Porter Brothers Store worth $6,988 (as a comparison value)

Snapshots of the "Barbary Coast Contingent"

A Sells Floto circus came to town and there gave its complete performance, from the gala parade in the morning, main performances afternoon and evening, ending with the after-concert at night.

Rhyolite turned out en masse–the Four Hundred of Nob Hill, the Barbary Coast contingent from Amargosa Street, and Indians from miles away joined "just folks" to make circus day one of the biggest days of the boom days.

...[Another day], *while the desert tenor, who was also the superintendent of the Sunday school, was singing "Rock of Ages" at the Sunday school gathering holding its session in the schoolhouse on the hill, girls recruited from San Francisco's Barbary Coast were loudly singing "The Holy City" and "When the Sands of the Desert Grow Cold" in the big corner saloon at Broadway and Main Street.*

–Betsy Ritter of the *Rhyolite Herald*

1907 Tax Assessments in Rhyolite
The Adobe Saloon and Dance Hall estimated at $2,600
Alberta Dent's brothel (formerly Maggie Keely's) estimated at $3,500, including $800 worth of diamonds
Mabel Vaughn's Jewel Consolidated estimated at $7,400, including a $150 diamond ring
Henry Duval owns seven lots on the east side of Amargosa Street housing mostly cribs and one brothel, estimated at a total value of $7,825
The entire workings of the Montgomery Shoshone Mine (not including mineral rights) estimated at $6,400

The years 1906 and 1907 were good for the inhabitants of Rhyolite overall, and its tenderloin was thriving. Population growth was steady, and the economy continued to prosper, despite being hard hit by fallout from the 1906 San Francisco earthquake.

A Mother's Prayer

A very charming lady came to the Hotel with a little girl about nine years old and asked the landlady for a room for the child, also wanting her to sort of look after her. The landlady at once said the new school teacher has a room here and perhaps she would take her over. We had a nice talk and I offered to see that little Virginia was cared for during waking hours. She also said I will see she has every earthly thing she needs and you, too. Well, I wouldn't take anything and was glad to have her company when out of school. The mother then said Virginia doesn't even know I am in the camp and I don't want her to ever know as I have a cottage of ill fame. I cared for Virginia the best I could and, believe it or not, every night the mother would go into the room and kneel in front of her bed for a prayer. She told me her life story and it was very sad. Finally, Virginia found out where her mother was and in a few days they both disappeared.

—Rhyolite schoolteacher Louise Presser

By 1908, however, a variety of factors had combined to doom the booming metropolis to ultimate failure, and though the population peaked that year at a number some estimate to be about six thousand, it quickly began to dwindle.

First and foremost among these factors was probably the shaky footing of the Montgomery Shoshone mine, a fabulous producer that had helped put Rhyolite on the mining map. Many other smaller mines were already played out, and a rush to the nearby new camp of Pioneer drew many citizens of Rhyolite on to what they hoped were richer prospects (they weren't).

On Amargosa Street, conditions were slipping from exuberant prosperity to a worrisome economic limbo. That year, the tenderloin was especially hard hit first by the murder of Mona Bell, as all eyes turned to the red-light district and a campaign was launched to wipe out what the *Bullfrog Miner* called "the species of so-called men who live off the earnings of fallen women: pimps and 'macques' to be more explicit." Like most such frenzies, this one soon died out, but the residents of Amargosa Street were already struggling with a downturn in their fortunes.

That August, a fire broke out on the upper west side of Amargosa Street and destroyed several substantial buildings, including the Jewel Consolidated. By then, Mable Vaughn could see the handwriting on the wall. She relocated to San Francisco and never rebuilt on the same scale. Eventually, a small string of cribs replaced the Jewel, but the days of elegant brothels on Amargosa Street were over. Henry Duval, a French immigrant who owned the largest share of property in the tenderloin, continued to operate a brothel and string of cribs for several years, but these were more moderate facilities, lacking the style and opulence of the Jewel.

The numbers below illustrate the decline of property values along Amargosa Street. This decline generally mirrored the larger devaluation of property in Rhyolite as a whole:

1908 End-of-the-Year Tax Assessment
The Adobe Saloon $1,800
Henry Duval $4,950
Alberta Dent $1,400
Mable Vaughn $825

1909 End-of-the-Year Tax Assessment
Bob Bynum's Estate (Adobe) $1,050
Henry Duval $2,730
Mable Vaughn $225

1910 End-of-the-Year Tax Assessment
Henry Duval now owns ten lots, including the Adobe Saloon, estimated total value $2,210
Mable Vaughn $120

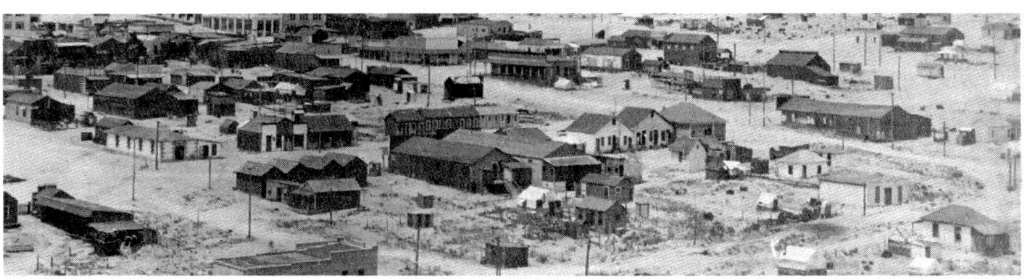

Rhyolite's Amargosa Street in 1909. After the 1908 fire burned the larger brothels to the ground, a string of cribs took their place. *Courtesy of Central Nevada Museum.*

In 1910, the census taker found Henry Duval still living on Amargosa Street with a small number of female "lodgers" in one of his brothels. The population of the tenderloin by then had dwindled to fewer than twenty identifiable inhabitants, most living in less than sumptuous conditions. The hundreds of women who had plied their trade in the town's restricted district had dispersed to places like Tonopah, Goldfield, Pioneer or other parts of Nevada and California.

By 1911, even Henry Duval had moved on to Las Vegas, though he continued to hold on to his property until the mid-1920s, perhaps hoping that Rhyolite would rise again.

Mable Vaughn also apparently clung to that dream for some time, keeping her property until 1914, when she allowed it to revert to the county to settle a $4.96 tax debt.

Rhyolite's red-light district, along with the rest of the town, then began the long, slow process of reclamation by the desert wind and sun. Author William Carruthers visited there on New Year's Day 1926 and wrote in his book *Loafing Along Death Valley Trails*:

> *I made a camp fire in Rhyolite's empty streets and beside it tried to sleep through a biting wind that seemed aptly enough a dirge. The next morning I poked around…to marvel at things of value left behind…The cribs still bore the castoff ribbons and silks of the girls and for all I know, the satin slipper which I found on a bed may have been the one that Shorty Harris filled with champagne to toast the charms of Flaming Jane.*

Today, the only real remnant of the old red-light district is the crumbled foundation of the old Adobe Dance Hall, the first substantial building erected in the Rhyolite tenderloin and the last to give up the ghost.

Chapter 7

THE LIFE AND DEATH OF MONA BELL

A little after midnight on January 3, 1908, Rhyolite night watchman Harry O'Brien walked down Golden Street, past the darkened windows of the Cook Bank and Porter Brothers Emporium and along Colorado. He stuck his head in at the doors of several saloons as he made his way toward Amargosa Street. There, in the heart of the tenderloin, the city came alive at night with loud music from the dance halls, boisterous singing, jostling foot traffic and the keening of roulette callers in the saloons. But that night, above the usual din, O'Brien heard a commotion at the Mission Bar, a frame saloon next door to the Adobe Dance Hall.

He stepped in to investigate. Neither of the women who had just bought half shares in the business, two dance hall girls known as Norma and Skidoo Lil, was in evidence. But Norma's boyfriend, a volatile gambler named Fred Skinner, was drinking with some of his friends and roughhousing, smashing up the bar. O'Brien ordered them to settle down and moved on.

Another three hours would pass before O'Brien, now coming out of McDonald's Saloon at the corner of Main and Broadway, heard frantic shouting. Hurrying toward the sound, he met a drunken Skinner running down Main Street wearing only his union jack underwear, blood streaming from his chest. "I shot Norma," Skinner cried, "and Norma shot me. I want to make a confession."

And that marked the end of the short, turbulent life of a woman the *Tonopah Bonanza* newspaper called "as hardened a denizen of the red light district as ever came to Rhyolite." It wasn't an uncommon story, at least not

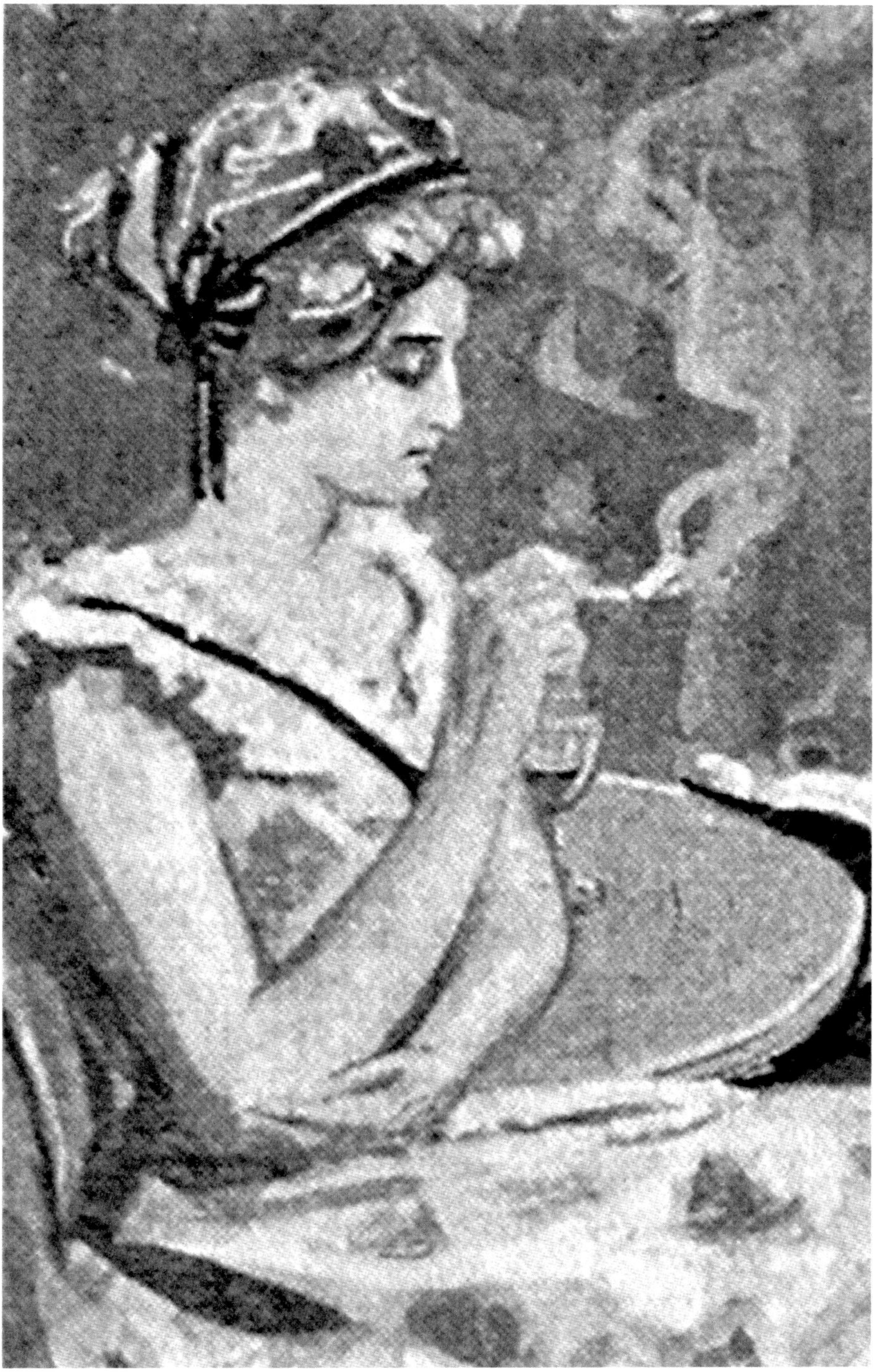

An illustration of a dance hall girl smoking a cigarette, circa 1910.

in the details leading up to that awful night. Women like Norma could be found in the Nevada mining camps by the hundreds. As a prostitute lodged on the lower rungs of the tenderloin social ladder, working out of cheap cribs and dance halls, she was one of many women whose identities and pasts were obscured by a variety of aliases and a habit of never remaining too long in one place. What became uncommon about her story, however, was how it ended and the fact that her notoriously public death made possible the telling of the tale of her life.

Norma first arrived in Rhyolite in early December 1907, not long after her twentieth birthday. The town was nearly three years old, and its red-light district was well established. The Jewel Consolidated was the palace of this societal microcosm and offered truly lucrative employment to the right kind of woman. But by then Norma had already chosen a different path. Like many prostitutes who began their careers in a boomtown tenderloin, she started out with a bit of a handicap—a crafty, smooth-talking man riding on her skirt tails. With Fred Skinner in her orbit, Norma would never make it past the front door of a place like the Jewel. However lovely and fun the slim, dark-haired Norma might be—and there were many who spoke of her good looks—her relationship with the violent, volatile, hard-drinking gambler kept her marginalized even in this already marginalized community. And there were some who later claimed that Fred had not held her back so much as he had pushed her into the life in the first place. After all, they said, she had not been like this before she met him.

Norma first came into the world on October 20, 1887, in the small town of Battle Creek, Nebraska. The name her parents gave her was Sarah Isabella Peterman—Sadie for short. Emery and Carrie Peterman had met and married in Iowa farm country and then migrated in steady increments through Nebraska and South Dakota before settling in Seattle, Washington, when Sadie was about fifteen. Emery supported his family of nine children, of whom Sadie was the fourth, working as a carpenter in the Seattle shipyards.

Little information survives about what Sadie's girlhood might have been like, aside from the regular moves from place to place. Her parents attended meetings of the Christian Science church and were said to have been sober, hardworking, unexceptional people. Sadie's eldest brother, Chauncey, worked as a reporter in Washington for the *Tacoma Times*.

Sadie graduated from Ballard High School in 1906 and soon after met a man named Clinton Columbus (C.C.) Heskett, eleven years her senior, of whom her parents did not approve. But Sadie was largely governed by impulse, and before long, she had eloped with Heskett to the piney forest town of Chadron, Nebraska, where they were married that same year. Sadie was already practicing the art of obscuring her identity, and although she was over eighteen, she lied about both her age and her mother's name on the license application.

From Nebraska, the couple moved on to Colorado, where they settled in Arrow, a rowdy, short-lived railroad town with a predominance of saloons and a healthy red-light district. But at that point, according to one account, Sadie, who now insisted on being called the more grown-up name of Isabel, was a model wife who stayed dutifully at home when she was not attending church.

Perhaps in those days—though it seems unlikely—Sadie Isabel intended to settle down to a quiet domestic life. If so, she had apparently chosen the wrong man. Heskett, though he later denied any guilt in the matter, was sought for forging checks in the name of a local saloonkeeper and found it convenient to leave town in a hurry. On his way out, he asked a friend of his, a stocky, swarthy, twenty-nine-year-old gambler named Fred Skinner, to keep an eye on Isabel. Despite his rather unprepossessing appearance, complete with a gold front tooth, Skinner was a charmer capable of inspiring confidence and admiration in other men and was magnetically attractive to women.

Born Llewellyn or Wellington Felker on a modest farm in Barton, Vermont, in November 1878, one of the youngest of about ten children, Skinner had

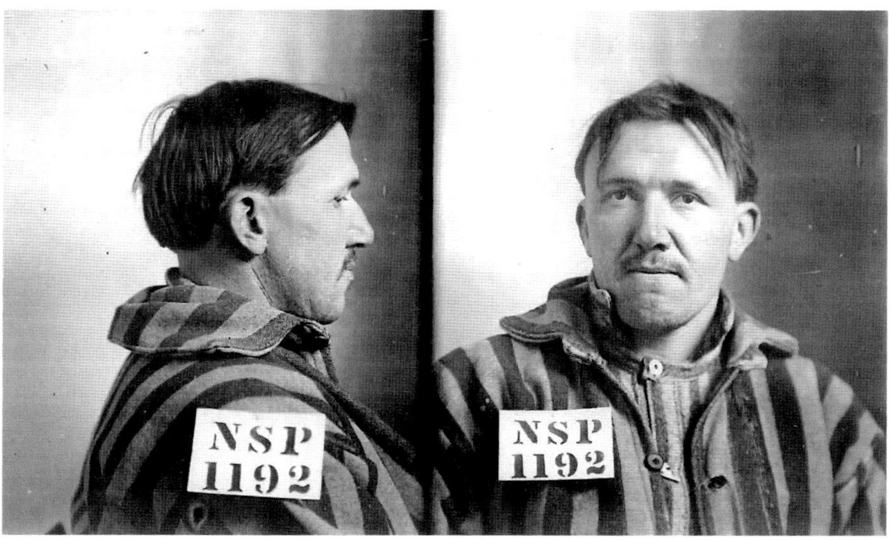

Fred Skinner's prison mug shot after the murder of Mona Bell, 1908. *Courtesy of Nevada State Library and Archives.*

already packed a great deal of adventure and mayhem into his young life. After a brief grammar school education, young Llewellyn traveled across the country alone to become an engineering apprentice to his brother Albert Felker in Seattle, not far from where the Petermans would later settle.

Prior to the outbreak of the Spanish-American War, according to Albert, Llewellyn enlisted in the navy and sailed out of San Francisco. After a couple years of active duty and some brief combat, he was discharged at the end of the war and went to Butte, Montana, where his mother and sister, Sarah Cunningham, were living.

That spring, Sarah, who was nearly full-term pregnant, was attacked and badly injured by her husband with a knife. A few days later, when the husband returned to attempt a reconciliation, Llewellyn and his mother refused to leave Sarah's bedside. When the husband leaned over Sarah, ostensibly to give her a kiss, Llewellyn would later say that he saw the gleam of a knife. Without waiting to investigate, he stepped forward and shot Cunningham dead. Felker served fifteen months in a Montana prison for manslaughter before his conviction was overturned in 1903. During his incarceration, he was part of a sensational prison break with five other men and later surprised authorities by turning himself in.

By the time he met Isabel, he had changed his name to Fred Skinner and was drifting around Colorado as a gambler. He had also acquired a wife named Anna, who was then living in a little house in the coal mining town of Walsenburg, Colorado, and taking in sewing to pay the mortgage while her husband indulged his wanderlust.

Sketchy accounts of the personalities of both Fred and Isabel indicate that they were less than emotionally stable, both perhaps inclined to the dramatic. If since her marriage Isabel had been carefully suppressing the streak of restlessness that colored her personality, in Fred she found an outlet. Before long, the two had fallen in love with an all-consuming passion that gave no quarter to their spouses, their commitments or any notion of propriety. She accompanied Fred into Arrow's red-light district and drank with him in the saloons, apparently becoming belligerent and combative on occasion. Her first brush with the law happened here, when she was reportedly arrested for vagrancy. She pleaded not guilty, demanded a jury trial and was turned loose.

Fred and Isabel left Colorado together in the middle of July 1907 and headed for the Nevada boom camps. In those days, central Nevada was bustling with promise and restless excitement as large numbers of people hastily stuffed their belongings into a suitcase or two and chased the most

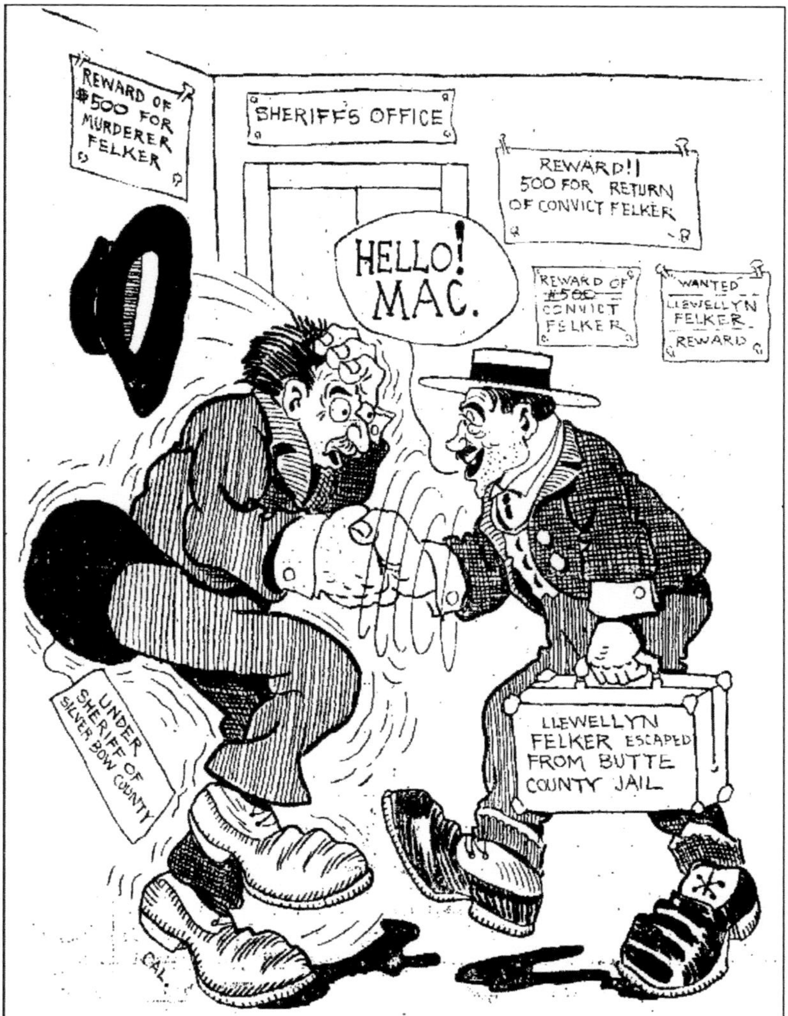

Society Note—Mr. Llewellyn Felker, after a pleasant vacation trip through th Olympia mountains, has returned to Butte.

Llewellyn Felker surprised the warden at the Montana State Prison when he returned of his own accord after a sensational prison break in 1902. *Courtesy of the* Anaconda Standard.

recent gold or silver strikes from town to town. Fred and Isabel were soon caught up in the whirlwind.

It was probably in Fallon, Nevada, that Isabel began working as a prostitute. By the time they reached the camp at Manhattan in October 1907, she had gained a certain amount of experience as well as a new name. Calling herself Mona Bell, she rented a crib that opened into the Parlor Saloon in Manhattan's red-light district and went to work. Fred began running poker games at several saloons in town.

Isabel had become estranged from her parents since leaving Colorado, but she continued to maintain contact with her family through her younger sister Mildred. She kept letters her mother had written her tied with a ribbon in a bundle at the bottom of her trunk along with some family photographs and took them with her each time she moved to a new camp.

By the time she and Fred hit Manhattan, things were less than easy between them. Mother Levy, who owned the Parlor Saloon, would later testify that she witnessed Fred being abusive to the girl Mona while they lived in her rooms but conversely that he also doted on her and often slept in a room adjoining her crib, separated from Mona and her clients by only a thin board wall.

In early November, a fifty-two-year-old miner named A.G. Cable spent the night with Mona Bell, paying her twenty dollars for the privilege. In the morning, when he woke up broke, he asked if he might have ten dollars of it back as a loan. Mona refused. "I didn't feel like lending him ten dollars when I didn't know him any better," she said later, "but I had five dollars in silver, and because he was an old man and because he'd been nice to me, I gave him five dollars in silver to pay his hotel bill."

Later that morning, Cable blew his brains out in the lobby of his hotel, and Mona Bell, Mother Levy and Fred (now using the last name Davis) were all arrested on charges of robbery. A friend of Cable's, a drunken, unreliable miner, said he thought Mona had taken $400 from the man, and the loss had driven Cable to that desperate act. For lack of any substantial evidence, Mother Levy was soon released, but Mona and Fred spent over two weeks in the county jail awaiting a grand jury hearing. It was suggested that Fred might somehow have been involved in Cable's death, but he denied it. Ironically, Fred's testimony included the following statement: "I never threatened to kill anybody or inflict harm on anyone…I was in no bad mood whatever, and even when I am in a bad mood I never think of killing anyone."

Fred and Mona were both released on November 21. The luxury of freedom was short-lived for Fred, however. Angered by what he claimed was the judge's unreasonable decision to bind him and Mona over to the grand jury, Fred planned revenge. While being escorted by the judge from the courtroom to the jail, Fred lured the older man, whom he knew had a weakness for drink, into a bar. Fred bought a round, toasted the aging judge and then punched him squarely on the jaw, knocking loose several of his

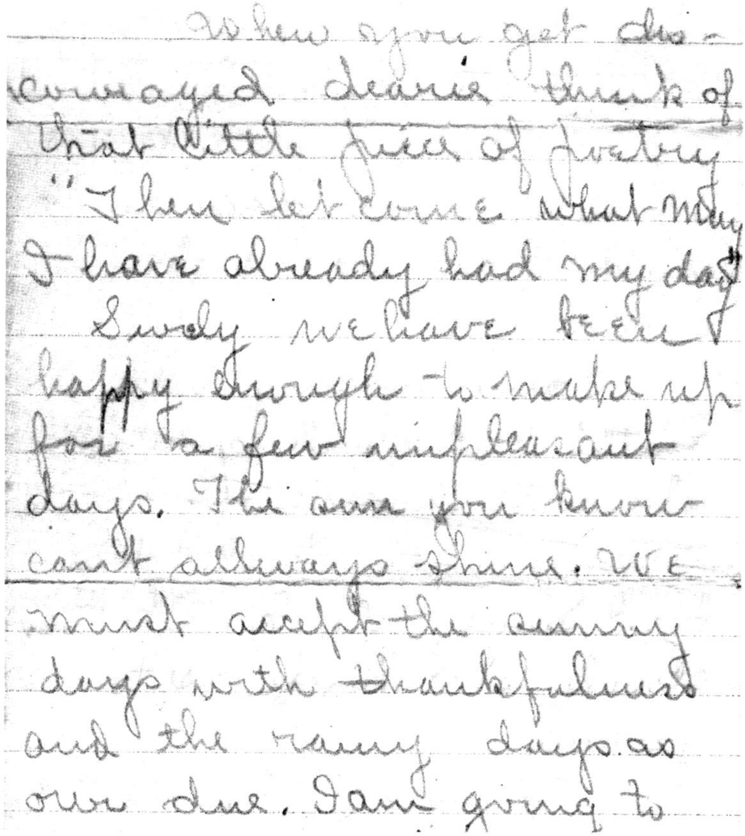

when you get dis-
couraged dearie think of
that little piece of poetry
"Then let come what may
I have already had my day
Surely we have been
happy enough to make up
for a few unpleasant
days. The sun you know
can't allways shine. We
must accept the sunny
days with thankfulness
and the rainy days as
our due. I am going to

A page from the letter written by Mona Bell to Fred Skinner while he was in jail in Tonopah. The letter quotes a few prophetic lines from Tennyson's *Maud*: "Let the sweet heavens endure, / not close and darken above me, / Before I am quite sure that there is no one to love me, / Then let come what may, / to a life that has been so sad, / I shall have had my day." *Courtesy of Nevada State Library and Archives.*

teeth. As soon as the grand jury cleared Fred and Mona of the first charge, Fred was rearrested for assault and sentenced to serve sixty days in the Tonopah jail or pay a $300 fine. Mona moved on to Rhyolite in search of work, hoping to make enough money to help pay Fred's fine and secure an early release.

"Surely we have been happy enough to make up for a few unpleasant days," she wrote to Fred at the jail. "The sun, you know, can't always shine. We must take the sunny days with thankfulness and the rainy days our due. I am going to work down there and get you some kind of work and we will be quite happy." She added, "If I can get any other work when I get into a new town it's no more tenderloin for mine. It doesn't pay."

But she quickly changed her mind. In Rhyolite, Mona changed her name to Norma, found employment at the Adobe Dance Hall and soon became known in the tenderloin. "She drank and smoked and swore like a pirate," one newspaper writer later recalled, and "her vocabulary of profanity was picturesque to the limit." But later, the thing people would most remember about her was that by then, as lovely as she was, her eyes seemed cold.

When Fred was released in early December, he went back to using the name Skinner and joined Norma in Rhyolite, where they rented a two-room cottage on upper Main Street, a block and a half away from the red-light district. He pursued his career as a professional gambler, carrying dice and several packs of cards in his vest pockets. On about the first of January, Norma purchased a half interest in a saloon next door to the Adobe known as the Mission Bar. Her business partner was another red-light resident known only as Skidoo Lil, who had probably also worked at the Adobe.

On the last night of her life, Norma went out on the town with Fred and two other men named Bion Demmings and Frank Wright. They had a meal in one saloon, drinks in another and a crème de menthe in a third before making their way back to open the doors of the Mission Bar. Norma was lagging behind that night and said she didn't feel well, and Fred became irritated with her. At the bar, he insisted she drink a glass of beer, but she didn't want to. He kept at her until she finished it, but she balked at drinking the foam. Enraged, Fred threw a glass at her from the other end of the bar, striking her on the shoulder, and then another, striking the hand she put up to defend herself. Then he closed in on her and hit her with his fists until she dropped to her knees. As she begged him to stop, he kicked her while her friends looked on, mortified but too frightened of Skinner to intervene.

Norma struggled to her feet, broke loose of Fred and ran for the door, but he followed her and kicked her again, calling her such foul names that later Demmings would refuse to repeat them in front of a female court reporter. When Fred's rage abated, almost as quickly as it had come, he released Norma, and she asked for permission to go home. When it was granted, she kissed him goodnight and left the bar quietly.

Later, after the bar closed, Demmings walked home with Fred. On the way, he worked up his courage and ventured that he didn't think Fred should beat Norma so severely.

"F—k her," Fred answered. "She is used to that."

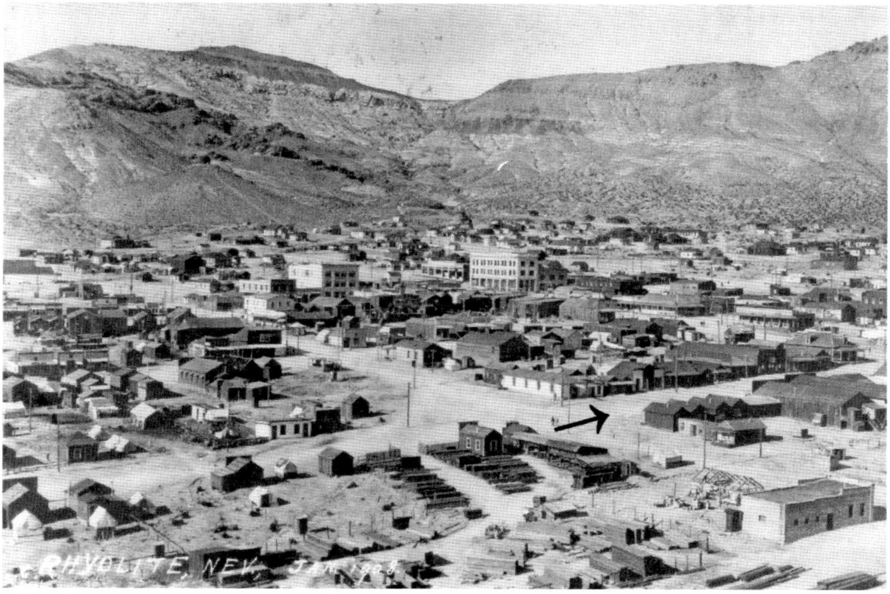

Rhyolite's Amargosa Street, 1908. The Adobe Dance Hall stands at one end, the Jewel Consolidated at the other. *Courtesy of Central Nevada Museum.*

When Demmings dropped Fred at the cottage on Main Street, Norma came to the door in her white cotton nightdress and said goodnight. It was the last time anyone other than Fred would see her alive. Inside, he and Norma settled down with more liquor, drinking and talking and consumed perhaps another pint before the trouble started. Later, Fred claimed that the subject of their conversation was his wish to give up the life he was leading and return to his wife in Colorado. He said he'd made up his mind while sitting in jail at Tonopah, where his eventual release was secured in part by money his wife provided. But he hadn't wanted to tell Norma this, he said, because he feared her temper. He claimed she had threatened many times to kill him if he tried to leave her.

That night, when he told her of his decision, she went wild, he said. She attacked him, but he pushed her away, and then she reached for a pistol on the nightstand and shot him twice before he could wrest it away from her. When she turned away to reach for another pistol on a shelf above the bed, he said, he knew the only way to stop her from killing him was to shoot her before she had a chance. He fired three shots, hitting her in the neck and back and killing her instantly. He then ran out of the house and down the street, where he met up with Officer O'Brien.

"I shot Norma and Norma shot me!" he yelled. "I want to make a confession."

But after Skinner calmed down, sobered up and realized that his wounds were superficial and not likely to prove fatal, he changed his mind about the confession. He dragged O'Brien back to the cottage, where he hovered over Norma's prone corpse; kissing her; straightening out her legs, which had buckled beneath her when she fell; clearing the matt of dark hair away from her face and cutting off a lock of it to put in his pocket; and saying he wished it had been him instead. Meanwhile, during these maneuvers, he managed to hide the gun that had killed her. Finally, O'Brien got Fred dressed and took him to jail.

By a little after daylight, a crowd was gathering outside the cottage, though Norma's body had been removed to Bacigalupi's Undertaking Parlors. There, Bacigalupi's assistant found a multitude of bruises and cuts all over her body, indicating she had been beaten on more than one occasion before her death. A rumbling could be heard all over town by the outraged and horrified citizens, and a lynching was talked of in many quarters. Norma might have been a "hardened denizen of the red light district," but she was also a small, attractive woman whom many wanted to believe had been led astray and ruined by Fred. Every chivalrous instinct in the male population was aroused by the manner of her death and especially by Fred's claim of self-defense. They eyeballed this broad-shouldered, heavy-set man who used his fists on old judges and small women and began sizing him up for a rope. The sheriff quickly removed him to Beatty and then to Tonopah for safekeeping until he could stand trial.

Meanwhile, Emery and Carrie Peterman received a telegram in Seattle notifying them of their daughter's death. Carrie Peterman wired back to Rhyolite that officials should contact C.C. Heskett, now in Fallon, Nevada. Apparently, since learning that his wife had run off with Fred Skinner, Heskett had been searching for her, regularly reporting the results of his endeavor to the Petermans. Heskett came on the run to Rhyolite, where he was met with sympathy and kindness from the officials in charge of the case. His coming to collect the body of his dead wife was romanticized by the local press, and when he testified briefly at the coroner's hearing, the papers lauded his manly grief. Before many more days had passed, he boarded a Washington-bound train with the body, escorting Isabel back to her family. She was buried quietly in the Peterman family plot at the Crown Hill Cemetery in Ballard, Washington, and the grave was marked only with a small, plain, crudely lettered cement slab. Later, Fred told his brother that he turned over all the cash and possessions he had at the time of his arrest to the family to help pay the costs of the funeral.

Anna Skinner, the wife Fred left behind in Walsenburg, Colorado, apparently harbored no ill will and soon arrived in Tonopah, where she worked as a seamstress to support herself and help pay Fred's trial expenses. Once, during the court proceedings, she rushed the police guard to give her husband a kiss. Fred's elder brother Albert Felker, to whom he'd been apprenticed as a teenager, also arrived and attended the trial, doing what he could to help Anna raise money.

Selecting a jury to try Fred Skinner proved difficult, as there were few men in any of the surrounding camps who would not readily admit to a bias against him. Many, including Deputy District Attorney Paul Delaney, believed Fred had shot himself to bolster his claims of self-defense. "Brazen brute, you," said Delaney, addressing Skinner directly during his opening statement at the trial, "you who sit there and smile into the faces of men, why do you not hang your head like the cowardly dog you are and crouch and cower and whine like you did when you thought you had shot yourself too deep? Oh, that a noose had been placed about your neck for some of your former crimes before you selected this poor girl as your victim and destroyed her honor and sent her soul unprepared to meet its God!"

A letter from Mona to Fred while he was in jail indicated that the wild jealousy Fred spoke of and the fears that one of the pair would leave the other were all his own. "Dearest," Mona wrote, "you should try to brace up and trust me. I wouldn't have gone this far if I hadn't intended to stick to you…No matter what anyone thinks of you I know you to be truly good. I know you have the most loyal heart that beats in a human breast and most of all you are the only man in the world for me."

Delaney and chief prosecutor Pat McCarran easily convinced the jury of Skinner's guilt. In late March, Fred was convicted of first-degree murder, condemned to life in prison—a sentence many thought too lenient—and transported to the Carson City penitentiary to begin serving his time. After the sentencing, Anna Skinner moved to Carson City to be near her husband, but she divorced him in 1911.

Over the next seven years, Fred would appeal the case four times, eventually succeeding in having the sentence reduced to fifty years. In 1912, he escaped from Carson City but was recaptured in San Francisco three weeks later. When he became eligible for parole in 1917, Carrie Peterman and two of Sadie Isabel's sisters wrote a letter expressing their wish that

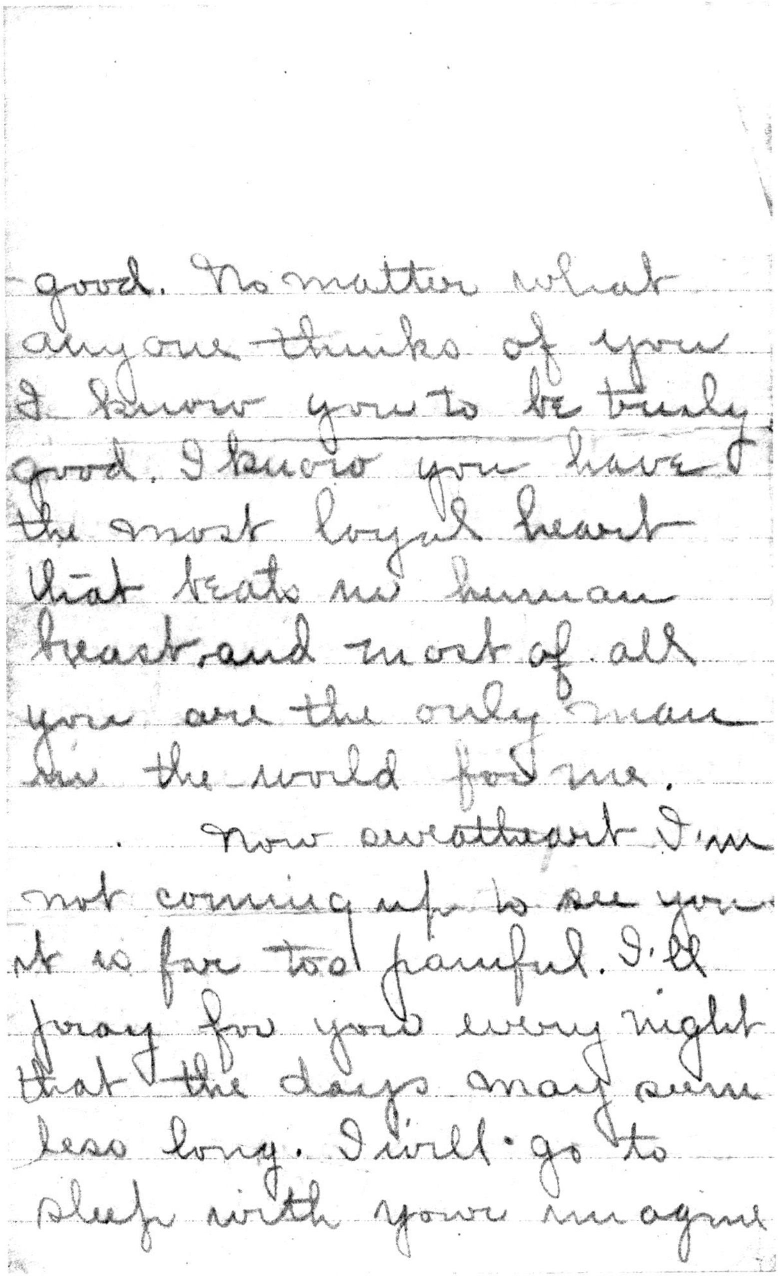

good. No matter what
anyone thinks of you
I know you to be truly
good. I know you have
the most loyal heart
that beats in human
heart, and most of all
you are the only man
in the world for me.
Now sweetheart I'm
not coming up to see you
it is far too painful. I'll
pray for you every night
that the days may seem
less long. I will go to
sleep with your image

A letter written by Mona Bell to Fred while he was in jail in Tonopah. The letter, found among her belongings, was introduced as evidence at the murder trial. Although Fred claimed that Mona was jealous and dangerous, in the letter, it is she who tries to calm his jealous fears. *Courtesy of Nevada State Library and Archives.*

parole be granted and that he "should be given another chance among men." However, Fred would not see a free man's light of day until 1923. That year, Emery and Carrie Peterman sent a telegram to the Nevada Board of Pardons asking that Fred be granted a full pardon. He was paroled to his brother in Los Angeles three days later.

Fred was ideally suited for life in the Prohibition era West. He continued to operate under a variety of aliases and to charm both men and women

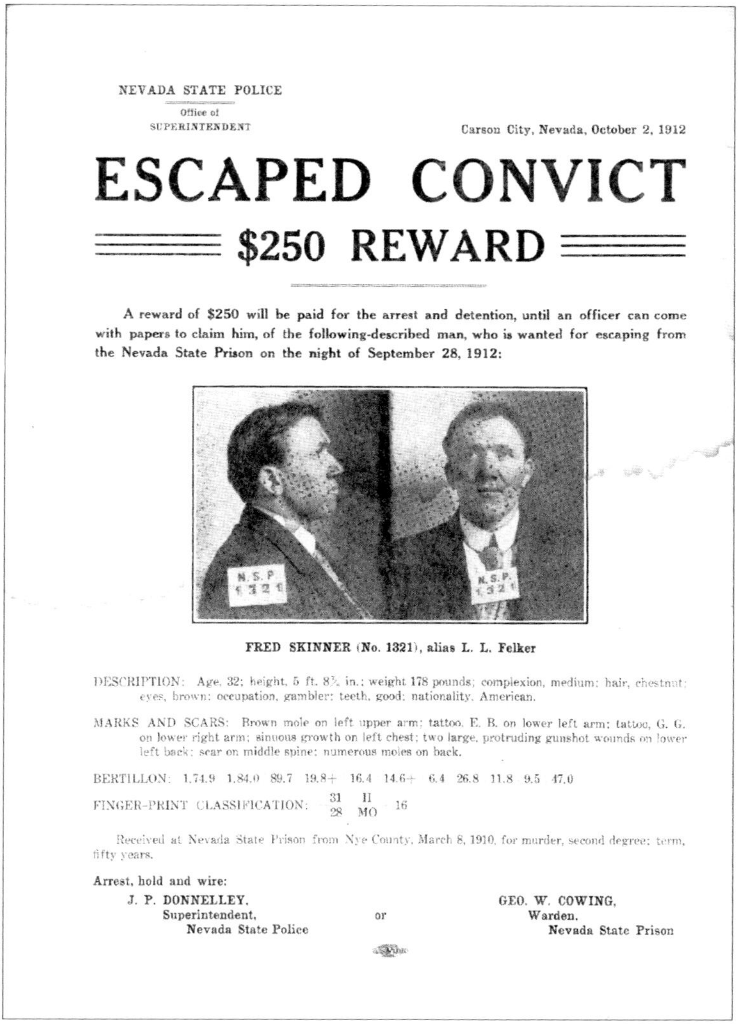
NEVADA STATE POLICE
Office of
SUPERINTENDENT

Carson City, Nevada, October 2, 1912

ESCAPED CONVICT

$250 REWARD

A reward of $250 will be paid for the arrest and detention, until an officer can come with papers to claim him, of the following-described man, who is wanted for escaping from the Nevada State Prison on the night of September 28, 1912:

FRED SKINNER (No. 1321), alias L. L. Felker

DESCRIPTION: Age, 32; height, 5 ft. 8½ in.; weight 178 pounds; complexion, medium; hair, chestnut; eyes, brown; occupation, gambler; teeth, good; nationality, American.

MARKS AND SCARS: Brown mole on left upper arm; tattoo, E. B. on lower left arm; tattoo, G. G. on lower right arm; sinuous growth on left chest; two large, protruding gunshot wounds on lower left back; scar on middle spine; numerous moles on back.

BERTILLON: 1.74.9 1.84.0 89.7 19.8+ 16.4 14.6+ 6.4 26.8 11.8 9.5 47.0

FINGER-PRINT CLASSIFICATION: 31/28 II/MO 16

Received at Nevada State Prison from Nye County, March 8, 1910, for murder, second degree; term, fifty years.

Arrest, hold and wire:

J. P. DONNELLEY,
Superintendent,
Nevada State Police

or

GEO. W. COWING,
Warden,
Nevada State Prison

A wanted poster showing Fred Skinner as he looked in 1912 when he escaped from the Nevada State Prison. *Courtesy of Nevada State Library and Archives.*

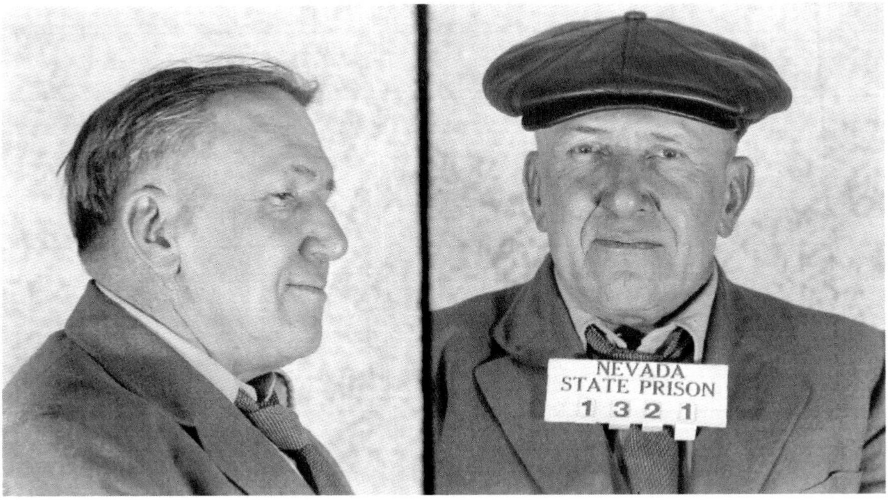

Fred Skinner's (later known as Roy "Doc" Russell) mug shot from 1935, when he was arrested for bootlegging in Las Vegas. *Courtesy of Nevada State Library and Archives.*

alike. In 1925 and 1926, he was wanted for burglary by the Los Angeles Police Department but managed to evade arrest. In the late 1920s, he married a young woman named Ruth many years his junior; fathered three children, all girls; and became involved in one of the largest bootlegging operations in Las Vegas under the alias "Doc" Russell.

But he never really learned to control his temper, and in 1936, he was arrested for assaulting his seventeen-year-old foster daughter, dragging her out of a neighbor's house by the neck when she refused to come home with him. The girl got her revenge a few years later when called upon to testify against him in ongoing investigations into his bootlegging activities. This landed him back in jail, and his second wife also divorced him. He was again paroled in late 1938 and continued to live in Nevada for several years. The last trace of him, a brief mention in his sister's 1961 obituary when he was about eighty-two years old, showed him to be living in Vancouver, Washington, less than two hundred miles from Sadie Isabel's grave.

"An interesting angle to the man's personality," wrote prison warden William Lewis about Fred in 1937, "is that in spite of his inclination to boast of the men he has killed, he is industrious and very active...He is smart and keeps busy all the time building for the future. He must be around the sixties, but you'd never guess him beyond 45 years. He will never grow old."

And neither, of course, would Sadie Isabel.

Epilogue

Many years after the death of Mona Bell in Rhyolite, when the town had mostly been reclaimed by the desert winds and sun, a woman named Mrs. Herschel Heisler was running a curiosity and rock shop out of the old train depot, selling ghost town souvenirs to curious travelers. To liven things up a little for her visitors, she decided to take poetic license with Mona's story and built a false grave for her out on the edge of town. Because poor Mona worked as a prostitute, Mrs. Heisler told sympathetic tourists, she had not been admitted to the regular town cemetery. The grave, and its story, remained long after Mrs. Heisler was gone. Today, it is brightly decorated with beads, high-heeled shoes and other small tributes such as liquor bottles and cigarettes left by visitors. A small group of women gather at the grave once a year to hold a ceremony and honor Mona Bell.

A Night in the Life of Mona Bell

Following is the transcript of testimony taken from Mona Bell, F.E. Davis and I.C. Levy in Manhattan, Nevada, on November 5, 1907, before the couple came to Rhyolite. This unusual document, edited for brevity and readability, allows Mother Levy and Mona Bell to describe in their own words an average night at work.

I.C. Levy, being first duly sworn, testified:

My name is Mrs. Levy, sometimes known as Mother. I live down here in the first house in the tenderloin district, run the saloon down there, the Parlor Saloon. When I first saw Mr. Cable and Mr. Lawrence, they were standing at the corner of the house outside talking very loud, which attracted our attention, and the lady [Mona] says, "Mother, there is some one out here that is talking out here, go and see who it is," and I looked out of the door and I couldn't see very good so far away.

I don't see very good, so I went down to the corner of the house; "Oh," I says, "this is Mr. Lawrence," I says, "how do you do, come in." And at that they both came in and we sat down, on the piano stool, Lawrence did, and the other gentleman sat on a chair, and the young lady sat down on his lap and asked him to buy a drink. He didn't, he says, "No, I don't care to drink," and then she asked him if he would go to her room, and he said "Yes," and

Turnabout

Some five months after Isabel Heskett's death, another couple fell to quarreling in a red-light saloon in the new camp of Rawhide. Jack McDougal had recently relocated from Rhyolite, where he kept a saloon called the Butler. He soon became involved with a woman named Leslie Noman, owner of the Tanaan saloon in the Rawhide tenderloin. That Saturday afternoon in May 1908, McDougal was drinking heavily and arrived at the Tanaan in a foul mood. He began badgering Leslie and kept at her, growing steadily more abusive. Eventually, much like Fred Skinner on the night of Isabel's murder, Jack threw a beer glass at his lover, hitting her in the face. Unlike Isabel, Leslie had had enough of this kind of treatment. She grabbed a revolver from behind the bar and shot McDougal through the abdomen. He died three days later, and Leslie was acquitted of any criminal charges after witnesses testified that she acted in self-defense.

he went to the first room, the one that adjoins the saloon, that has a door from the saloon into the room.

And then she opened the door and says, "Mother, bring us a bottle of beer, he's going to buy a bottle of beer," and I brought a bottle of beer and he gave me $20 to change.

I didn't have the change, I sent out to get it, and he says, "Bring my change."

And I says, "Just as soon as it comes back."

We all sat down in that room and drank that bottle of beer until the change came back, and Lawrence says, "How much change did you give him?"

I says "$18—a bottle of beer $2."

And he says, "That is alright." With that the old gentleman and this lady went into her room and that is the last I ever saw of the old gentleman.

At 12 o'clock Mr. Davis came into the saloon and I told him Mona was busy, he said, "That is all right."

I says also, "The room that you're in the habit of sleeping in sometimes is occupied."

"Well," he says, "there's plenty of beds up town," and he says, "I'm not in a hurry."

I says, "There's no use of you going up town, I can't go to bed, you might just as well sit around and talk." And he sat down in the room and of course we heard the conversation in the other room all the while.

He must have remained there as long as an hour or more, and then he went out and says, "I believe I'll go out and get a little lunch, I'm hungry." And of course the kitchen stands out in the back of the house in the yard a little ways, and he went out and got lunch, and then he came out in my part and says, "Will you call Mona to come to lunch?"

I went and rapped on the wall and says, "Mona, come to lunch." And she says, "Alright," and the old gentleman says, "hurry back." And she came into my part and they both went out and got lunch.

While Davis and Mona went into their apartment for lunch Mr. Cable remained in the other room. They remained in the lunch room, oh, I should judge 20 minutes. Then Davis came back into the room and Mona came back also, but she left and went back into her room.

Davis never left the room after that till 6 o'clock in the morning. I heard Cable leave somewhere about 5 o'clock, soon after Lawrence left. I didn't notice whether it was daylight or dark, I have my curtains all drawn down and of course electric lights are burning, and I couldn't see whether it was daylight or dark.

I heard no complaint from Cable at his departure. Anderson slept in the other room next to the bar-room until 4 o'clock, then he got up and dressed himself. I happened to look in the room, I heard him, I says, "What are you getting out so early for?"

He says, "I've got to go to work."

I says, "Will you come and take a drink?"

And he said, "Yes, I will take a little whiskey."

And I poured out a drink, and as I did so Mr. Davis stepped out of my room and says, "Call the rest to have a drink."

I says, "Mona, won't you and your friend come in and have a drink? Mr. Lawrence is going away."

And Mona says, "No, he doesn't care for any."

So Mr. Lawrence had his drink and Mr. Davis had his, and Mr. Davis paid for it. I says to Mr. Lawrence, "You had better wait and take your friend with you, he's got to go on the stage at 6 o'clock."

And he made some remark, "To hell with him, let him come when he's ready." And went out at that, and that is all that was said. So then Mr. Davis and I sat in my room again and Cable went away, and I called Mona to come, it was cold in her room.

I says, "Come in and get warm." We sat there till six. We had a couple of drinks.

I says, "It is six o'clock, I haven't slept all night." They went to her room and I heard them talking till seven, and then of course I must have dropped to sleep and at 8 o'clock we wakened again.

Mona Bell takes the stand and states as follows:
Q: What is your name and age?
A: My name is Mona Bell, and my age is 20—20 the 5th of October.
Q: Where were you born?
A: I was born in Nebraska.
Q: Where do you reside and how long have you resided there?
A: In Manhattan, Nevada, for it is almost a month, it is a month, I cannot tell exactly.
Q: What is your business and profession?
A: I stay in the tenderloin district.
Q: You are a sporting woman?
A: Yes sir.

Judge Chambers: Now give any explanation you may think proper of the circumstances appearing in the testimony against you and state any facts which you may think will tend to your exculpation.

Mona Bell: Well, Mr. Cable came down, I should think about ten o'clock, and he stayed in the saloon a few minutes. He didn't buy any drink in the bar room, and he went in the next room to the bar room and bought one bottle of beer and gave Mother a $20 gold piece for it. He got $18 back in change. It was a $10 gold piece and a $5 gold piece and the rest was silver.

Then he went, he wanted to stop with me that night, and went into my room, and, well, he was in there I don't know just exactly how long it was. He bought two bottles of beer, which made $6 that he spent for beer. Then this man that was with him, his name is Mr. Anderson, I didn't know him at the time, came to the door of my room—there is two outside doors to my room, and asked to borrow $5 from Mr. Cable, and he gave him the $5 gold piece. Then after a while he called through the partition, Mother called through the partition, and told Mr. Cable that his friend wanted to buy her a bottle of beer and could he buy it and borrow the money from him. He said yes, and she came in and got the $2 from him there—she came to the door.

Then in the morning all that was said about any money when he woke up, he didn't seem to feel out of sorts, and he said "I want $400 of this Bank." That is all that was said about $400, and he asked me if I would lend him money, ten dollars, on his watch and chain. I told him that the watch and chain weren't any good to me, and that I didn't feel like lending him ten dollars when I didn't know him any better, but I had $5 in silver, and because he was an old man and because he'd been nice to me, I gave him $5 in silver to pay his hotel bill with. He had a ticket to Tonopah, he said he wanted to buy a drink while he went up the street, and in the morning when he woke up he wanted to know where the Merchants Hotel was, and said that was where he had left his grip.

He gave me $20 for stopping there and he bought three bottles of beer while he was there and he lent $5 to this friend of his, $7 altogether, $5 at one time and $2 at another; and he said that he wanted this $5, that he could get money in Tonopah, that the money he had here was tied up in the State Bank. He said he would pay me back the $5 that he borrowed when he came back.

Chapter 8
DIAMOND TOOTH LIL

THE MOST RECKLESS GIRL THERE EVER WAS

Pomona, California, 1963

On a sunny autumn day in 1963, an old woman sat under a shade tree in the yard of a Southern California nursing home, talking to a reporter. By then, she was a ward of the state dressed in cheap, frumpy clothes, a chain-smoking, recovering alcoholic. But life for Evelyn Hildegard wasn't always this way.

"I used to have diamonds on every finger and draped around my neck," she told the reporter, "now I'm down to this." Smiling, she pointed to her left front incisor, where one small diamond glittered in the afternoon sun.

For this was the notorious Diamond Tooth Lil, a woman who crisscrossed the country performing in dance halls from New York's bawdy Bowery to San Francisco's Barbary Coast and then worked the last great mining boom camps of the West. In those days, she was so lovely, so lively and bold that one small boy who met her would remember her for the rest of his life as the prettiest woman he'd ever seen. And an infamous gunslinger would spend almost forty years pining and searching for her after she slipped away from him in the lusty, rowdy smoke and haze of a Nevada boomtown.

Decades before, in the time when she was young and jostling for her place in the world of the chaotic mining camps, there had been in Death Valley a newspaperman named Carl Glasscock. He met her in the short-lived copper camp of Greenwater and prophesied, with a typical newsman's cynicism, that she would die a young and miserable death. But Diamond Tooth Lil lived

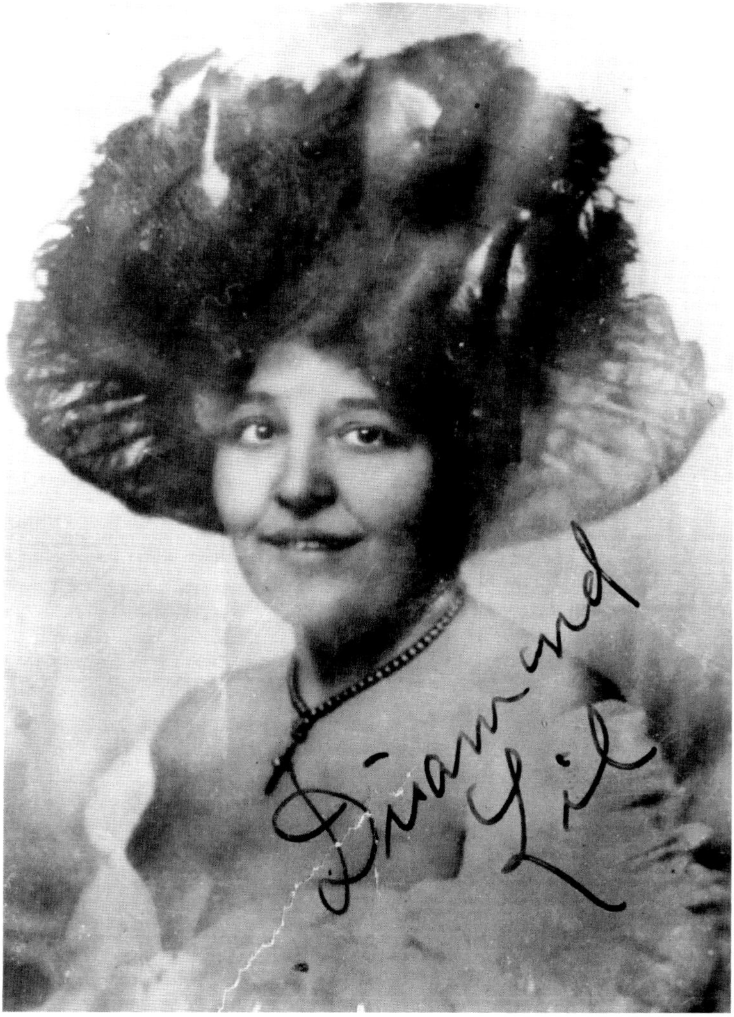

Taken about 1918 in San Diego, this photograph is the best-known and most recognized image of Diamond Tooth Lil. She gave wallet-sized copies of this portrait to people she liked or wished to befriend and had a large version of it hanging in an oval frame in her home in Boise. *Courtesy of Idaho State Historical Society.*

long and prospered, mistress of her own destiny, pleased with the memories of her past. Unrepentant to the end, she held on to those memories like the most precious of treasures and in later years used them to help create and promote her own legend with a zeal and vigor any boomtown speculator would have envied.

RED LIGHT WOMEN OF DEATH VALLEY

In the mining camps of Death Valley and central Nevada during the post-turn-of-the-century glory days, there were prostitutes, dance hall entertainers and madams galore. Many of them were beautiful, many had personality and flamboyance, many ran honest, upscale houses. But only one would find her way out of the murky historical mist enshrouding their lives and make a place for herself in the mainstream of history. In later years, as her contemporaries died off or faded into an invisible respectability, Diamond Tooth Lil flaunted her past and managed to become a western legend. But getting there wasn't easy.

When she first arrived in Death Valley country, she was a relatively obscure dance hall singer with a powerful set of lungs; a lush, curvy figure; and a penchant for fancy clothes. In that, she was no different than the hundreds of women already on the scene. What made her stand out was, perhaps, simply the forceful nature of her personality and her own desire to be noticed. In the end, the people who had been there, in Greenwater, Goldfield and Rhyolite, remembered her because she wanted them to.

She carried a gun, she smoked cigars, she wore a diamond in her tooth. She impressed herself upon their memories with a force of will unequaled by her peers, many of whom worked to erase their pasts as time marched on. Many wanted anonymity, wanted to be forgotten—and therefore perhaps forgiven—but not Diamond Tooth Lil. She was at once unrepentant and devoutly religious, tenderhearted and fierce tempered, never apologizing for her choices or backing down from a fight.

Blessed with a temperamental mixture of brash recklessness, a soft heart and a burning desire to succeed, Diamond Tooth Lil never appeared to see herself as tainted or less deserving of a good life. Because she never judged her own choices and believed until the very end that God was looking out for her, despite what anyone else might think, she had no need to hide her identity or justify her life. This left her free to capitalize on her past.

She reveled in the creation of her own legend, and later, that legend served as her reward. Long after she had given up the business of madaming, her status as a bona fide character of the Old West, helped along by the notoriety of Mae West's *Diamond Lil* stage play, made her a lively figure. And it supported her by bringing customers to her business ventures and later bringing reporters and historians to sit beside her while she told stories of the past.

But while she never tried to hide her past, even she, a seemingly open book, did have her secrets. In later years, when the woman known as Diamond Tooth Lil found herself courted by reporters and Old West historians, she often blurred the early details of her life. In honor of the memory of her mother and the family pride of her status-conscious older brother and to shield her own respectable daughter, she edited, embellished and edged around the facts of her beginnings.

Youngstown, Ohio, 1890s

Kathrine Fialla was born on September 29, 1885, in Iglo, Hungary (now known as Spišská Nová Ves), into a time of political upheaval. Five years later, her poor, uneducated Catholic parents, Michael and Teresia Fialla, along with a swarm of other immigrants fleeing Eastern Europe, would accompany her aboard a steamship bound for America. They were forced to leave Katie's eldest brother Michael behind until they could earn enough to cover passage for him. Of the ocean voyage, all Katie would later remember was that it was long and miserable, that there was never enough to eat and that her mother was violently ill.

But the Fiallas survived and made their way to Youngstown, Ohio, where Michael's brother got him a job in one of the many steel mills that kept the city shadowed in clouds of industrial smoke. The family moved into a cheap tenement apartment in an immigrant neighborhood, and the younger Michael made the perilous ocean voyage to join them. But life in America brought its own hardships.

While the Slovak-speaking Fialla children began the painful process of assimilation, for the elder Michael Fialla, life in Youngstown became unbearable. A new baby boy joined the family in 1894, but Michael was out of work, often drunk and branded a "worthless fellow" by the police officers who had frequent dealings with him. By the spring of 1895, he had become so abusive at home that Teresia swore out a criminal complaint against him. He was a kind man when he was sober, she said, but when drunk, he hit her with his fists. While confined to jail, Michael brooded until his dark thoughts drove him to attempt suicide with his own belt. In this he was unsuccessful, but within a day of his release, he had thrown himself in front of a fast-moving passenger train, leaving Teresia and the children to fend for themselves.

Railroad tracks hemmed in the industrial neighborhood where Katie lived, with coal and steel plants close enough to color the sky with their smoke and dust. The area was so dismal that one town reformer begged the city to provide a playground, lamenting, "There are so many obstacles [here] to thwart [a] child's growth." While their mother took in washing to support them, Katie and her brothers scoured the tracks looking for bits of coal that were left behind when loaded cars pulled away from the coal pile a few blocks over. These bits were fair game, unwanted, unnoticed. But one bitter cold winter day, the boys began climbing up onto the loaded cars and kicking down extra bits. It was a small thing but enough that Katie remembered it many years later as her first crossing over the line between the way her devoutly Catholic mother raised her and the way out of the drudgery that defined her existence.

In the fall of 1896, the pall of sorrow and misfortune that hung over them deepened when the baby Stephan, now two years old, died from injuries he sustained in an accident while in Katie's care. That same year, Teresia remarried to a man from her hometown in Hungary. John Knapic was a stern man, determined to rein in the growing streak of recklessness he saw in Katie.

But she was coming of age. She grew early into a woman's soft, round figure and discovered the power it gave her. When she was caught frequenting a local youth club pretending to be older than she was, her stepfather gave her "a beating with a strap that raised blisters on my behind," she later remembered. But jail, whippings and the threat of eternal damnation were as nothing in the face of Katie's determination.

While one brother went to school and worked hard and the other became a professional acrobat, Katie began stealing—small things she could sell to get money for the things she wanted. When she was caught and spent a week in jail, she said, her parents never once came to see her. But she didn't hold that against them since "they were poor and ignorant and didn't know what to do."

She went on stealing and saved up enough money to buy a dress and a pair of shoes. "They must have been cheap and god-awful," she later told biographer Harry Sinclair Drago. "I thought they were wonderful. I didn't know any better. They were the first halfway decent things I ever owned. I've worn some expensive clothes since then, but they never meant to me what the first pink dress did.

"I guess Mama knew how I got the money to buy them. She just shook her head and said nothing. I guess she was getting ready to wash her hands of me. As for me, I knew I wanted something better out of life than what I was getting."

At fourteen, she ran away to Cleveland and took a job as a servant girl. For $1.50 a week, she rose every morning at 5:00 a.m., worked hard and fell into bed each night by 9:00 p.m. But drudgery didn't suit her, and within a few months, she had abandoned the job and was arrested for vagrancy on the city streets. Her fresh-faced prettiness and youth won her the admiration of a *Plain Dealer* reporter and the sympathy of the judge, who ordered her returned to her mother.

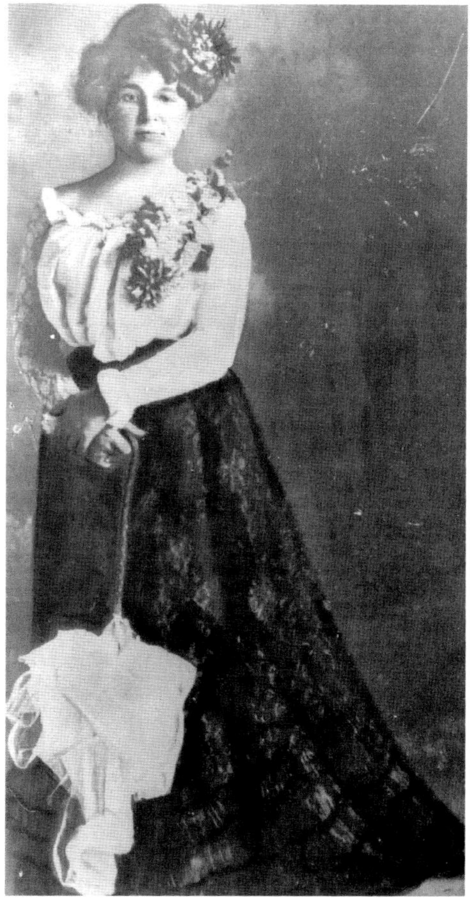

Kate Fialla, circa 1902. "This photo was taken in Chicago," she wrote on the back. "I arrived in California in 1902. This is the way I looked when I came here. I was 15." *Courtesy of Carrie Schikora.*

But Youngstown couldn't hold her then, and she soon ran away again. Years later, she told Drago that she had eloped with a flashy young man named Percy Hildegarde. They went to Chicago, she said, but Percy's family caught up with them and had the marriage annulled because Katie had lied about her age. Percy went home, but Katie stayed and went to work singing in the local dance halls. She had a hearty set of lungs and could make herself heard over the din of the noisy crowds.

Amid the smoke and noise, the "streetwalkers, pimps, small time gamblers and strong arm men," she found her place. In this unrestricted, wide-open world, she finally felt at home. She taught herself to play the piano and sang and danced and laughed and reveled in the romance and riches of her newfound life. Now subject only to her own whim, she traveled to New York, Chicago, San Francisco, Nome and Seattle and anywhere there was excitement and the promise of adventure.

Later she claimed to have sung at the St. Louis World's Fair in 1904, to have traveled with boxer Kid McCoy from Chicago and to have survived the San Francisco earthquake in 1906. When the Barbary Coast went down in flames, Katie headed for the excitement in the Nevada mining camps.

Goldfield, 1906

Katie had yet to take the fateful step of embedding a small diamond in her gold-capped right front tooth. She used a variety of names and liked to travel around, probably working in dance halls in towns like Reno, Carson City and Rhyolite, where she was remembered for her boisterous singing. By her own account, she worked as an entertainer on stage only in those days, but for entertainers and prostitutes alike, it was common practice to travel the red-light circuit from one place to another. The newer in town a woman was, the better money she could make.

In September 1906, Katie heard about the excitement brewing in the boom camp of Goldfield. Everyone with the means to get there was on their way to witness a highly promoted championship boxing match between Joe Gans and "Battling" Oscar Nelson. A brand-new boxing arena, still smelling of sawdust, stood ready for the big event, and over 100,000 spectators crowded in and around the ring.

Into this excitement, a town swamped with reporters and fight fans and men with money to spend, Katie arrived and sought out Tex Rickard at the Northern Saloon. Rickard, an old friend from her time in Alaska, told her to run through her music and be ready to work that night. "The most I was ever paid was in the Northern Saloon," she said. "Two hundred and seventy five dollars a week."

The rush of Goldfield suited her, and Katie decided to stay on. While socking away money on stage at the Northern, she cast an appraising eye at the brothels and dance halls in town and decided that she could do better. Calling herself Florence Hildegarde, perhaps in honor of Goldfield's rich Florence gold claims, she opened the Nevada Club on South Main Street in the heart of the red-light district. Among her customers were Death Valley Scotty, whom she said frequently paid for a drink with a twenty-dollar gold piece and told her to keep the change, and a notorious gunslinger named Diamondfield Jack Davis.

Whether Jack Davis was really the great love of her life, the one who captured her heart and she could never forget, is a matter of conjecture. In later years, it served them both to say so, and it was certainly true that at the time they gravitated toward each other like flames to an updraft. It was probably as a result of her association with him that she made the decision to have the diamond placed in her tooth. Wealth of any kind suited her, and Jack, if he wasn't dripping with it, was certainly mixed up in it. In those days, he swaggered around Goldfield draped with guns, a wealthy miner in his own

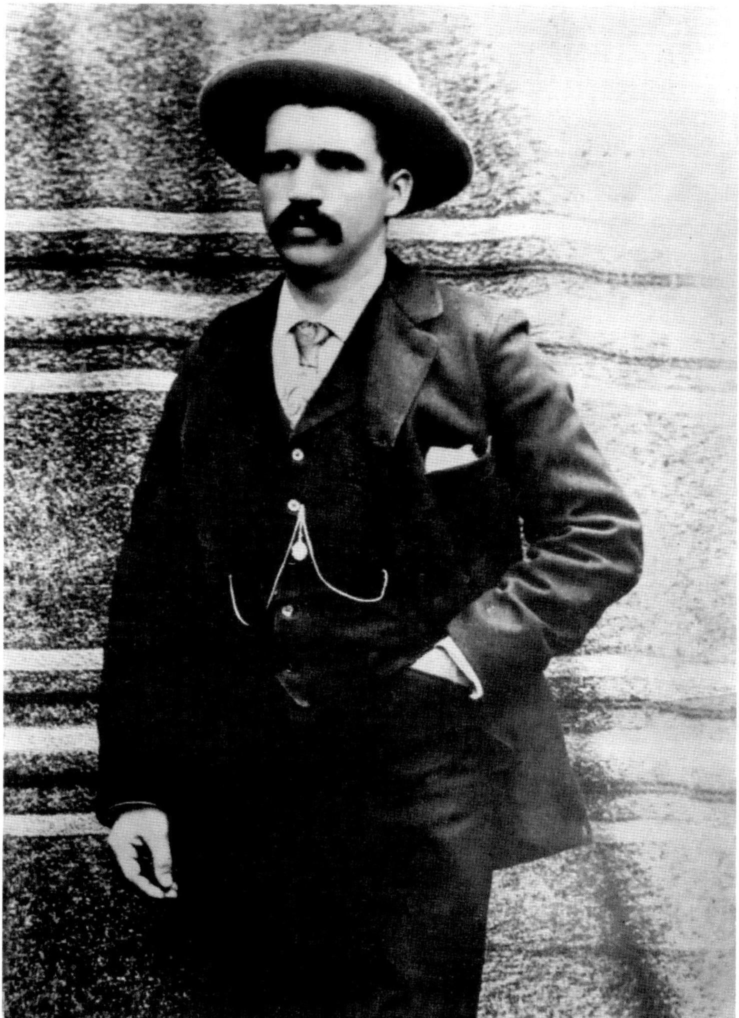

Diamondfield Jack in Goldfield, circa 1907. *Courtesy of Nevada State Historical Society.*

right and a hired gun for George Wingfield, one of the major stockholders in the fabulous Florence mine.

It was rumored later that Katie and Jack married, but in those days, he was already married to a young woman named Minnie. When Minnie filed for divorce, she would claim that Jack left her suddenly in the summer of 1907, about the time he and Katie took a trip together to New York City. It was also around this time that Katie acquired her famous ornament as

WE CAN'T HAVE THE NAVY IN GOLDFIELD BUT DIAMONDFIELD JACK HAS HIS ARSENAL

"DIAMONDFIELD JACK" DAVIS was born in Lynchburg, Virginia. Odd name that. Anyway, for 37 years Jack has been playing with a gun. At six months he began tetehing on the dull and deadly barrel of a six-shooter, and every time he gets mad now he whips out one of the four he carries and chews off a hunk of steel that soothes and satisfies him.

Some people in this wild west think Jack Davis is a "bad" man. He isn't. He's kind, and gentle and generous, and has a habit of behaving like sticky fly paper in warm weather when a friend is involved. In a pinch, I wouldn't be the least bit afraid of Jack, if I had the drop on him.

Jack Davis has had a romantic career. To look at him you'd never think that a dark-eyed damsel caused the first duel in which he engaged. But you know the old proverb—"still waters run deep." Well, it was down in Mexico, where the senoritas sing sweetly the lullabys of love, where the magic spell of romance rules with majestic wand; where 'tis better to love and lose than to just live. The aforementioned dreamy damsel whispered to Jack a tale that produced a fighting frenzy. We walked 'cross the floor, slapped a Mexican colonel, noted for his death-dealing duelling, on the face and immediately was challenged "to the death." They came to discuss weapons and Jack said:

"Shotguns at ten paces!"

That meant an undertaker for one at least and perhaps two. Jack didn't need his services, however.

Next we hear of Jack in Idaho. Everybody knows that story. How he killed two thieves in a fair fight, was tried, convicted and sentenced to be hanged, and in his "dying hour" was reprieved.

But the interesting part of Jack's Idaho experience was his discovery of the diamond fields. Hence "Diamondfield" Jack. Hence again our own Diamondfield, where lies the Daisy of the Desert, the Great Bend, with its Extensions and Annexes. Very few people are aware that "Diamondfield Jack" was "Diamondfield Jack" before the days of Diamondfield. But it's a fact. He brought ready made fame to the town and gave it a permanency even in those days of doubts.

"Diamondfield Jack" has been in every mixup, personal and political, since the gray-streaked desert began putting on dignified city airs. I am told that it is not prudent to call him "shorter and uglier" nor "particularly mendacious." Remember, he's a Virginian, and it's always best to smile when addressing him in the strenuous——— ——— ——— manner of the west.

A friend of Jack's asked him the other day why he carried four guns, and he replied:

"Well, if I ever got into a mix-up and didn't have my guns and got killed I'd never forgive myself as long as I lived!"

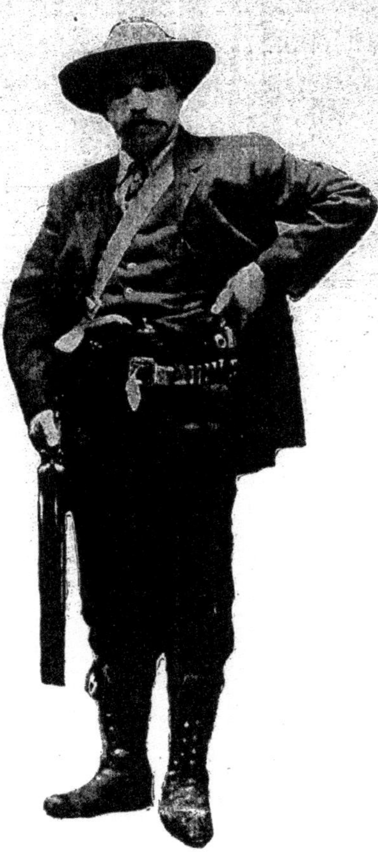

"Diamondfield Jack" Davis Drawing One and with One to Carry.

Diamondfield Jack cut quite a figure in Goldfield when he and Katie first met. Jack continued to live a colorful life, but by the time he reunited with Lil in Las Vegas in 1945, his fortunes had seen better days. In the last few years of his life, he worked in a Las Vegas casino and depended on friends for his living. He died in 1949 after a Las Vegas taxicab knocked him down on Fremont Street. *From the* Goldfield Chronicle, *May 2, 1908.*

the payoff for a gambling debt from a dentist in Reno, and the legend of Diamond Tooth Lil was born.

By then, word of the fabulous copper camp of Greenwater in Death Valley, and its rich investors, was everywhere. Diamond Tooth Lil probably

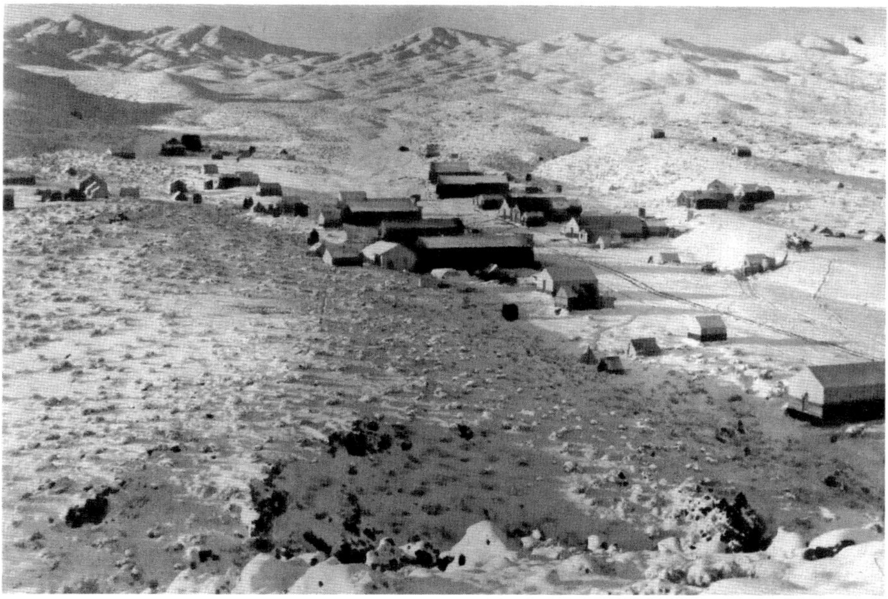

Greenwater covered in snow during the camp's first winter, when Diamond Tooth Lil was said to have found shelter for the women and children in the town's largest saloon. The larger tent buildings on the left of the main street in the center of town were both saloons. *Courtesy of Eastern California Museum.*

made her first trip to Greenwater late in the summer of 1907. Disembarking to take a rest at the stage stop run by Dad Fairbanks in Ash Meadows, Lil shocked Dad's fourteen-year-old daughter Stella by smoking a cigar and drinking with the men in the rough tent accommodations. Here she first met Dad's wife, Celesta, a devout Mormon woman with another daughter just about Lil's age.

Greenwater is the one place in Death Valley where Diamond Tooth Lil was well remembered, even immortalized in fiction and memoir, remembered also as Tiger Lil either for her fighting spirit or a dress she wore painted with tiger lilies. But it's also the one place she never mentioned in later years when she set about creating the legend of her past.

The camp of Greenwater was a failure, both in terms of its mining and business and also on a personal level for Lil. It began well, with Lil as the proprietress of the best "fair $5 house" in town. That winter she spent there was bitter cold, and one old miner remembered Lil sewing up a curtain to hang across the middle of the biggest saloon in town so that the women and children in camp could keep warm on the other side.

Tiger Lil in Greenwater, as remembered by Senator Charlie Brown:

> *Lil Lang, Mother Agnes and Tiger Lil came down* [to Greenwater] *from Rhyolite looking for greener fields and more money. They ran the three principal houses. Tiger Lil was a fine looking woman. She came into town wearing a beautiful dress with tiger lilies painted on it. Among the business people she was highly thought of. There was a lot of dealing in real estate and I heard Paul Wright, a broker, say, "I'd rather do business with Lil than anyone. She always lived up to her promise on any deal...One night down at Lil's place Red McCrimmon got abusive and started tearin' hinges off the doors. Lil ordered him out but he only got worse. Lil pulled out her shooting iron and it was shoot and jump, shoot and jump for 200 yards. Red never stopped running till he got uptown.*

But as the camp's fortunes failed, so apparently did Lil's. The portrait painted of her by the newspaperman C.B. Glasscock, in his "Gold in Them Hills," was of a woman whose fortunes had slipped considerably since she collected twenty-dollar gold pieces from Death Valley Scotty behind the bar of the Nevada Club. She had even, according to one report, been reduced to taking chickens in trade for her services.

Writer Elliott Clawson penned a fiction piece for the *Atlantic Monthly* in 1909 called "The Sheriff of Greenwater." The story depicted the town in vivid detail, and many of its fictional inhabitants closely resembled its real residents. He described a prostitute named Nellie who "had diamonds in her teeth [and] a quantity of hair, of two or three colors, which was wound carelessly around her head. Her face was pale and sickly, [and] she wore a loose calico Mother Hubbard."

If he'd based Nellie on a real person, he hadn't been favorably impressed by the original. This was not the vivacious beauty who had captured the heart of Diamondfield Jack. This was a young woman grown tired, a young woman worn out by the boom camp way of life. She was then only twenty-three years old.

Finally, Lil bid Ma Fairbanks goodbye and left Greenwater. Sightings of her were later reported from Death Valley Junction to Silver Lake and Cracker Jack as she apparently made her way down the Tonopah and

Tidewater (T&T) Railroad tracks, smoking her cigars, playing poker in the saloons and firing off her six-gun at anyone who crossed her. Fairbanks family legend tells that Lil eventually bounced back from her Greenwater slump and soon surfaced in San Francisco, where she purchased a corset for her friend Celesta and sent it to her through the mail. The two women would keep in touch, exchanging letters for the rest of Celesta's life.

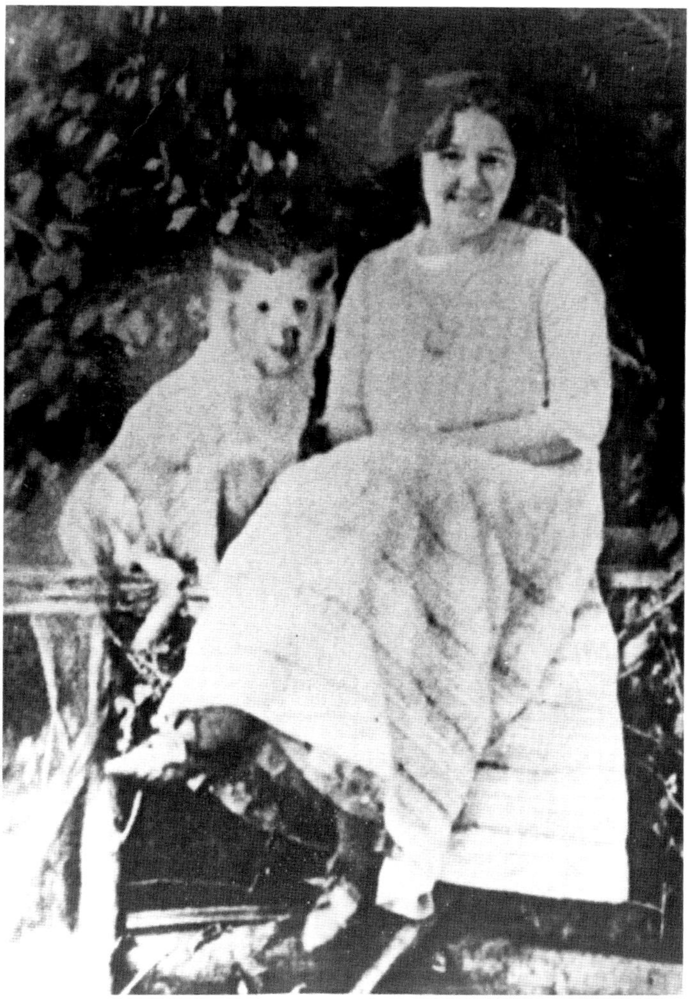

Katie Fialla at the Natatorium in Boise. "That dog," she wrote on the back of the photograph, "made a 50 ft. jump before I ever knew him. He does all kinds of tricks, he was with the Ringling Brothers once. He was given to me by George Mapleton, an ex-husband." *Courtesy of Idaho State Historical Society.*

Later on, Lil's memories of the hard times in Greenwater wouldn't jibe with the legend growing up around her. If she wanted to chronicle her life by its successes, Greenwater would have to be edited out.

Lil and Jack seem to have rekindled their flame for a while in Reno around 1908, when Lil established such a lucrative business that it was rumored the town bosses plotted to have her killed so they could take it over themselves. Whether this is what drove her from Reno or it was just a case of her habitual restlessness, she moved on to the small timber town of Lakeview, Oregon, where she was working out of a crib in 1910. Her career as a boom camp follower had officially come to an end.

Idaho, 1912

Lil spent the intervening years between Oregon, Washington and Idaho and was living in Boise by 1912, when she married a man named R.L. Miller in Mount Vernon, Washington. By then she was calling herself Evelyn, a name inspired by Florence Evelyn Thaw, a famous actress she saw briefly in Reno and whose dramatic personal life held some similarities to her own. From Washington, the Millers traveled to Texas, where she said her husband became mean and dangerous and that he even shot her once. She told Drago that it had taken the members of Miller's Fraternal Order of Eagles club to shield her and help her get away from him for good. What she didn't tell Drago is that when she left, she took a baby daughter with her. Frightened and exhausted, she returned to Youngstown for the first time since leaving as a teenager.

Youngstown was different now. The miserable tenement neighborhood where she grew up had burned to the ground in a labor riot a year or two earlier. Her elder brother was a prominent businessman and refused to have anything to do with her, but she was welcomed by the mother she adored. Once rested and her spirits restored, she returned to California. She took a job managing the Burnap Hotel in San Diego and used to walk to the beach with her daughter, where the cheerful toddler loved to ride on the merry-go-round.

They traveled to Arizona, where Evelyn married and left another husband, and then moved on again to manage another rooming house in El Centro, California, where Evelyn also briefly had another little girl under her care. But Evelyn was restless and had little faith in her own

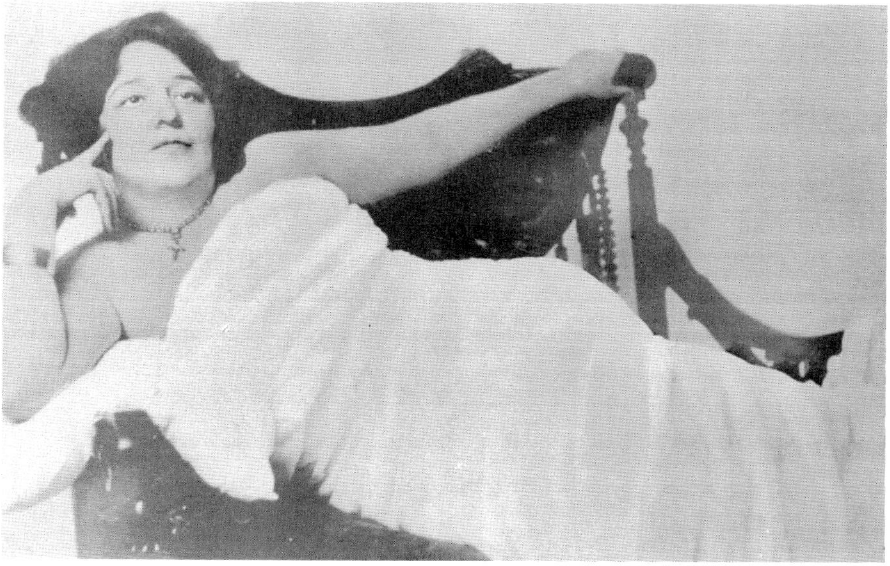

About 1918 in San Diego, where Evelyn Hildegard managed the Burnap Hotel for a short time. *Courtesy of Carrie Schikora.*

fitness for motherhood. Deciding that her daughter would be better off, she left the little girl in a Minnesota orphanage and fled back to Idaho, where she threw herself into business with an unparalleled vigor. In the years to come, perhaps to keep herself from dwelling too much on the past, she married at least four more times.

By the spring of 1920, she had settled in Boise for good. Doing business as Mrs. Evelyn Hill, she opened the Star rooms, known as a haunt of prominent Boise politicians in its heyday. Her reputation about town was generally good, but in 1922, she was arrested when one of the women who worked for her claimed Evelyn violated the nine-hour working law for women. In 1925, she was arrested again for keeping a disorderly house; she staunchly protested her innocence and asked for an opportunity to present her case. But she had friends in high places then, and the case was quietly dropped.

Lil never said what drew her to Boise, but it was the scene of a spectacular turn-of-the-century legal affray in which Jack Davis once cheated a hangman's noose.

Even so, she and Davis lost touch after Goldfield and didn't see each other again until 1945, when Davis, who said he'd been searching for Lil all along, happened to notice an article about her in a stray Boise paper. Their reunion in a Las Vegas casino where Davis was shilling for handouts made brief headlines.

Diamond Tooth Lil was a flamboyant figure in Boise, dressing in lavish costumes with feather boas and wigs to match. Her home was elegantly appointed with velvet hangings and expensive furniture. Naturally gregarious, she soon had a circle of friends and admirers, some of whom would stick by her for years. She married and divorced several husbands in Idaho in such rapid succession that she had to request an annulment for one wedding that took place before her last divorce was final. In 1933, she married what would be her last husband of record.

But while her romantic relationships never lasted and she had no inclination toward family life, her friendships with other women did endure. When she learned of another woman trying to break free of an abusive husband, Evelyn took her in. And as she aged, she enjoyed writing letters to her old friends.

By the 1930s, American popular culture had begun to romanticize the Old West, and Lil was happy to claim her place among its famous figures. The *Death Valley Days* radio program aired scripts including characters named Tiger Lil and Diamond Babe. And, too, this was the time when Mae West introduced her notorious character Diamond Lil. Because of the resultant publicity when West was arrested on a morals charge for producing the play, the name "Diamond Lil" made national headlines. The fame by association made Evelyn a curiosity and helped to keep her own Diamond Tooth Lil legend alive.

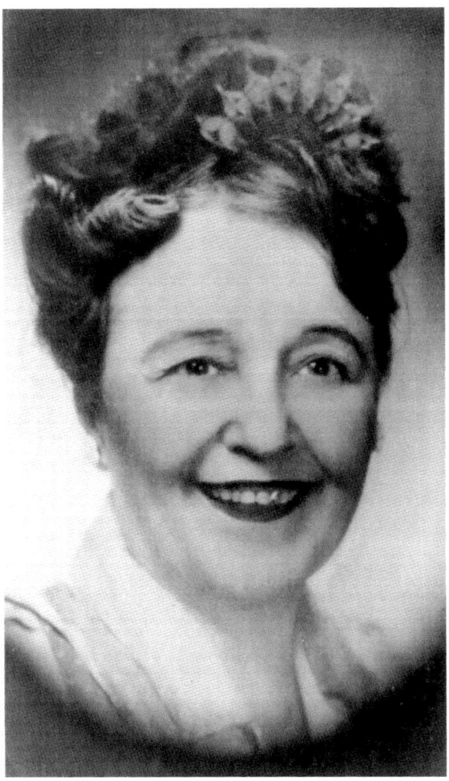

Evelyn Hildegard, around the 1940s, in Boise, Idaho. *Courtesy of Carrie Schikora.*

Evelyn had been in communication with Mae West at some point, hopeful that the two could join forces somehow. But West, who insisted that her Diamond Lil character had not been based on a real person, politely rebuffed Evelyn Hildegard. Among Diamond Tooth Lil's prized possessions was an autographed photo of West, but on the back she had written, "Here is the girl that turned her back on me. Well, this is L.A. Never be surprised at anything today. I'll give her credit, she done me a lot of good anyway so I haven't any kick."

By the 1950s, Lil had been immortalized by her friend William Carruthers in his book *Loafing Along Death Valley Trails*, as well as a host of other writers and reporters.

Epilogue

Lil's fortunes slipped as she aged. She ran brothels, bars, rooming houses and trailer courts, with each successive venture diminishing in scale and stature, until her status as a curiosity and a western legend was one of the only things that drew customers to her rundown establishments. "For the past twenty years I have been living alone, almost forgotten," she told an interviewer in the 1940s, "with an auto-tourist business to keep me busy and people to meet and talk to; people who undoubtedly look upon me as just another old lady, and little dream that I was Diamond Tooth Lil, the belle of the Barbary Coast.

"But not for anything would I change one moment of my life! Life always gave me what I craved and still does. I have money, friends, memories, and contentment…The old hectic days are gone—but my memories are sweet."

Although the auto court she ran on the edge of town boasted a log cabin that she recalled as the most beautiful home she had ever known, the Idaho winters eventually became too cold to bear. In about 1945, she left Boise and headed west to warm her old bones in the sun and join her younger brother John in California.

She had kept track over the years of her daughter, now called Betty, and made efforts to keep in touch with her by sending letters and photographs. But Betty, who had grown into a woman, did not return her affection or approve of Evelyn's life. She rebuffed Evelyn's advances, and the two never met again. But Betty would keep the photographs her mother sent and hand them down to her son one day with a brief and blurted explanation of his true lineage. In all the scandalous stories that Diamond Tooth Lil told to reporters and visitors and for all the memories she loved to relive, she kept Betty's existence a secret.

At first, life in California was comfortable. In 1954, Evelyn wrote to an old friend in Boise: "I am 67 now but I never feel old. Am always smiling. The

'Diamond-Tooth Lil' Now---and Then

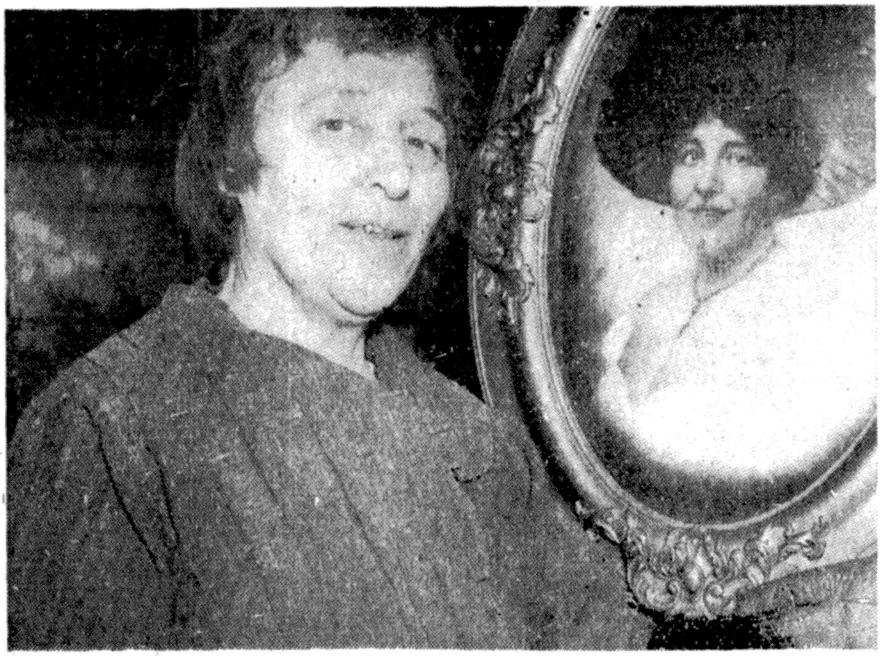

THIS PICTURE shows "Diamond-Tooth Lil," as she appears at her auto court in Boise today, her gem-studded front tooth gleaming as she smiles at her memories of a gayer age. A picture of her, as she appeared at the time when she was the toast of the dance halls, hangs on the wall beside her.

Diamond Tooth Lil in 1943, posing beside the famous photograph of herself in younger days. *Courtesy of the* Idaho Daily Statesman.

Master has one eye on me, as he keeps me in good trim. Many thanks to him, I never forget him. When Mother lived she prayed for me daily as I was the most reckless girl that ever was. I left home at 13 and you see I was in care of the Master for here I am in one piece."

Eventually, through heavy drinking and poor investments, Evelyn wound up a ward of the State of California, penniless and nearly blind. But residence in a nursing home suited her, she told a reporter in the autumn of 1963: "I've been every place I want to go and seen everything I want to see. So now I'm resting."

Lil spent the last few years of her life in the Claremont Sanitarium in Pomona, California. Toward the end, the nurses who attended her reported, the boisterous Lil grew silent. She had no visitors. She had outlived her contemporaries and had no close relatives nearby, no one left to whom she was dear. None of the nurses had any way of knowing that Betty, having

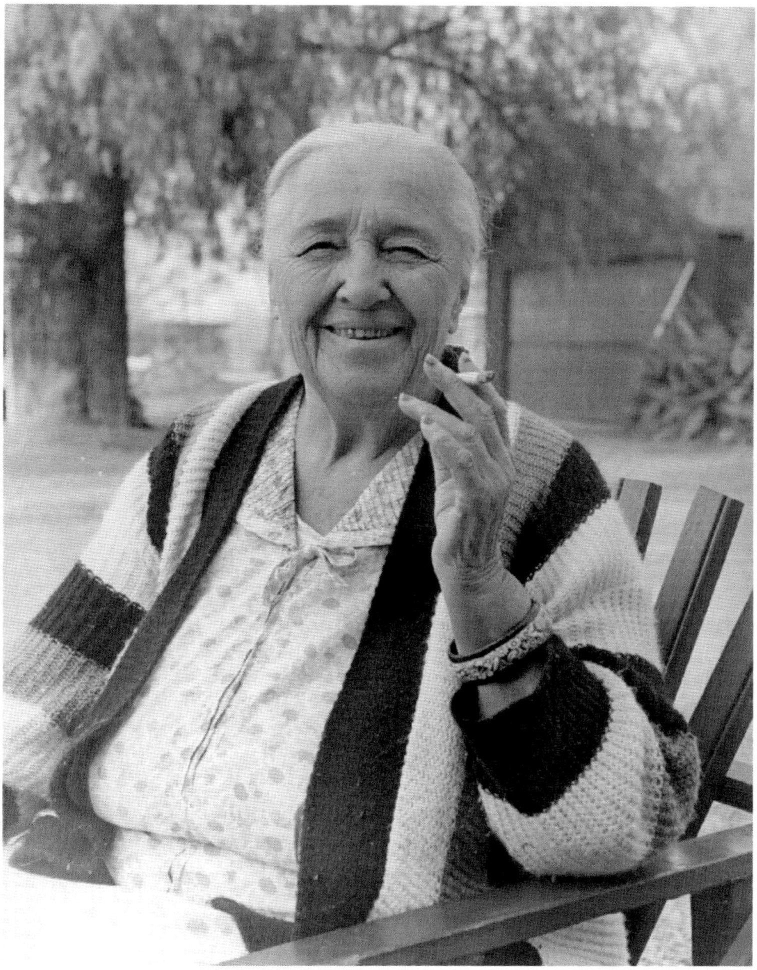

Evelyn Hildegard at the Pomona rest home, circa 1963. *Courtesy of Colorado Historical Society, Stephen H. Hart Library.*

discovered her mother's whereabouts, had actually come all the way from Seattle to stand outside the door to Evelyn's room one afternoon. But in the end, she had lost her nerve and gone away.

So, it seemed, Evelyn would simply fade quietly away. She had given up speaking, but on the night she died, nurse Ruth Osborne recorded in her journal that Lil sat up in bed and spoke quite clearly. The last words ever uttered by this famous western madam surprised those who heard them. "Hail Mary full of grace," she said and then laid back down in her bed.

This prompted Osborne to call the local Catholic priest. When he heard whose soul hung in the balance, he gathered reinforcements and came on the run with four parishioners in tow. They knelt around the bedside of Diamond Tooth Lil and prayed.

The next morning, at the respectable age of eighty-two, Evelyn Hildegard died peacefully and was later admitted for burial at the Catholic Holy Cross Cemetery in Pomona. No one knows what became of her famous diamond-studded tooth. Nurse Osborne remembers that Lil's stepbrother came all the way from Ohio hoping to take it with him, but Osborne believes that Lil was buried before he arrived and that the tooth—the sum total of all the wealth she possessed—was buried with her.

Although the last years of her life were spent in poverty and relative solitude, until the end Evelyn maintained that she never regretted trading in the dull, drab future of Katie Fialla for the fame and adventure of Diamond Tooth Lil. "It was rough, it was tough, but how I loved it!" she once said. "Not for anything would I change one moment of my life."

In 1932, C.B. Glasscock had surmised that the Tiger Lily must be dead. "A woman of her profession could scarcely have survived another quarter-century of mining camp life," he wrote. But he had underestimated the staying power of this remarkable woman who actually outlived him by some twenty years. Diamond Tooth Lil took control of her own legend and rewrote it to suit her vision. If storytellers of the time, like Glasscock, would chronicle her only by her failures, she would chronicle herself by her successes.

It was, after all, her life, and her story to tell however she chose.

The Diamond Tooth

So far as is known, Diamond Tooth Lil's famous ornament went with her to the grave. She had promised to will it to a children's home in Boise, Idaho, but died intestate as a penniless ward of the state. Most accounts by those who knew her say that Lil had her own teeth until she died, but a Boise dentist told another story:

> *Interviewer: Could you describe Diamond Lil to us or tell us a little about her?*
> *Thomas Lohrman Berry of the Quality Dental Lab, Boise, Idaho: Diamond Tooth Lil…run a rooming house down on Grove Street when I*

first knew her. And she said she won that diamond in her tooth—it was a gold crown with a diamond set in it—and she bet some dentist in Reno, Nevada, on a horse race. She won the bet and, by golly, she made him put the diamond tooth on. In 1946 she had her teeth pulled by Dr. Jeppson. And he sent that tooth over to the lab and wanted to know if we could put it in a plate, which we did. We made her plates, and we put in that crown with that diamond in it in the plate…I haven't seen her after she left here. I did have her plate in at one time. After 1954 she broke a plate and I repaired it.

INTERVIEWER: What size was the diamond in her tooth?

BERRY: I would say it was probably ¾ or maybe a carat. It was a pretty good sized diamond…It was [set in] *a gold crown. It was on a lateral, left lateral…the tooth next to the center tooth, between the cuspid and the center tooth.*

—interview conducted by the Idaho Historical Auxiliary Oral History Project, 1969

Chapter 9

A RENDEZVOUS FOR LOW-GRADE CHARACTERS

When the Pacific Coast Borax Company began pushing its Tonopah and Tidewater Railroad through the white-hot crags of the Amargosa Canyon in the summer of 1906, legend has it that the endeavor required three constantly rotating groups of men. First came the ones who were doing the backbreaking labor under a grueling sun; second, the ones who were throwing water on the first set to keep them alive; and third, the ones who were coming up behind to replace the men whose strength gave out or who quit while they could still walk away. And along behind them, on the back of a freight wagon with her husband and two little boys, rode a young woman on her way to the wide-open desert where she would one day become a legend.

Kitty Marbaker had come out west from Pennsylvania as a teenage mail-order bride only a few years before and married thirty-three-year-old Bob Tubb, an Arizona freighter and entrepreneur on the watch for the right opportunity. In 1906, he saw a chance to capitalize on the coming of a new railroad. Bob and Kitty Tubb and their two small children, Leon and Robert, set out for a barren, windblown bit of desert slated as the junction point for the T&T and its spur to the borax mine at the edge of Death Valley. They followed the T&T as the workers laid down its tracks, and when construction stalled out during the heat of summer, they traveled on ahead and filed a homestead claim to a piece of land south of the proposed spur and east of the main line route.

Seeing this, high-minded British officials of the Pacific Coast Borax Company became concerned about the tent saloon the Tubbs had erected and petitioned the Board of Supervisors of Inyo County:

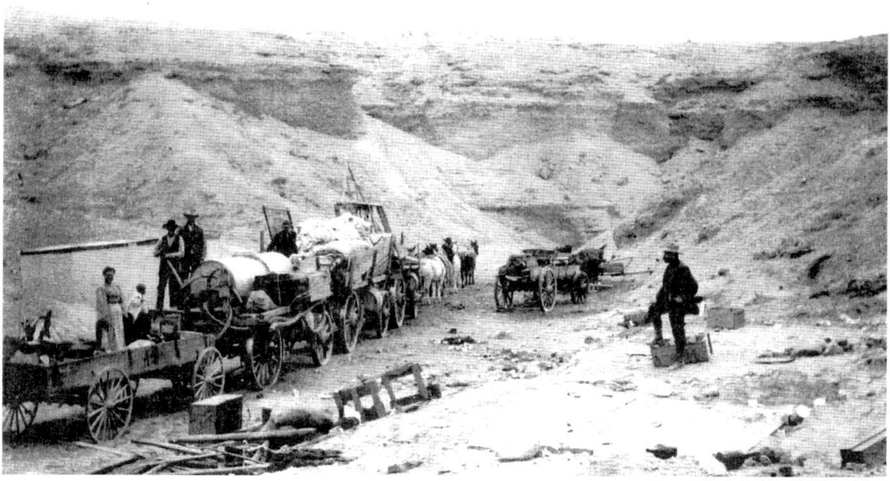

Kitty Tubb on the back of a freight wagon making its way through the Amargosa Canyon behind the T&T Railroad in 1906. *Courtesy of Nancy Tubb Peterson, Judy Tubb and Virginia Tubb Goodsen.*

> *We beg you to try to regulate the liquor traffic, so that it will be almost impossible for tents or saloons to either commence or do business along the line of our railroad in your County during construction…A saloon on this desert, especially the class of saloons that follow railroad construction camps, are nothing more or less than a rendezvous for low grade characters, women as well as men, whose only occupation is to fleece the working man by thieving or other criminal means.*

But the Borax Company's plea came too late, and soon Bob and Kitty were joined by all sorts of "low grade characters." Railroad workers and their families populated the small settlement, and they were joined at the Tubbs' place by miners and travelers. Borax Company man Harry Gower, who spent many years at the Junction, recalled, "Tubb's Saloon was an institution consisting of a saloon, desert store, food emporium, hotel, and, speaking plainly, a disreputable roadhouse—all operated by Bob Tubbs [*sic*], his family, and associated scoundrels of both sexes."

Kitty would hold the whip hand over the unruly crowd at the Junction for the next several years while her fierce temper and expert marksmanship earned her the nickname of Shotgun Kitty. She was in charge of the women who worked in the cribs behind the saloon and also of the restaurant. Wash Cahill, superintendent of the T&T Railroad, recalled that the Tubbs "sold an

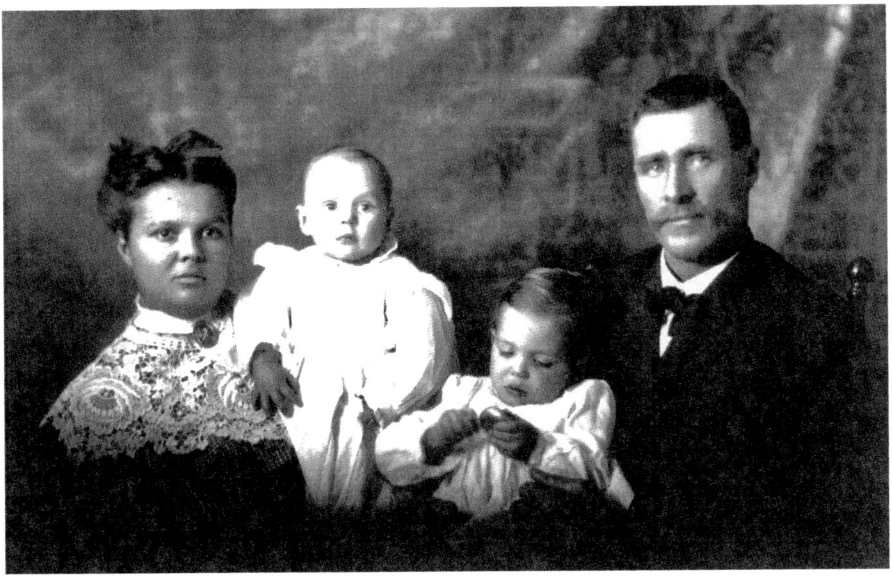

A family portrait of Kitty and Bob Tubb with their two younger sons before they moved to Death Valley Junction. *Courtesy of Nancy Tubb Peterson, Judy Tubb and Virginia Tubb Goodsen.*

occasional meal to weary travelers or semi-blind people who could not observe the sanitary conditions. Those who sometimes had to eat there and were in the know generally ordered boiled eggs in the shell and potatoes with the jacket on."

Back in those days, Cahill remembered, Tiger Lil often stopped by for a hand of poker on her way to some boom camp farther down the tracks. Women were scarce in the desert, and Lil's Greenwater confidante Celesta Fairbanks, now running a roadhouse in Ash Meadows with her family, had also formed a friendship with Shotgun Kitty.

In 1908, Kitty left the Junction to give birth to her third son, George, in a Los Angeles hospital, but the following year, when she went into labor early with her fourth son, Kitty gave birth under a mesquite tree near the site of what would later become the Amargosa Opera House. Danny was small and would never quite gain the robust good health of his brothers, who roamed wild with the children of the Mexican section hands in the days before a school was established. Fierce Kitty was protective of the small, weaker boy, and he would be her companion for the rest of his life.

And while Kitty's domestic responsibilities grew, so did business at the Tubb Saloon.

Despite the fact that the Inyo County government conducted its business on the far side of Death Valley, a day's ride away from the Junction, reports of unruly conduct there continued to reach officials. Among the county's efforts to mitigate the untamed revelry was the passage of County Ordinance Number 97, which barred women from saloons. This ordinance seemed to have had little effect on Kitty, but it did have consequences for a woman named Hattie Cook.

Cook opened a saloon at the Junction in 1909 with her partner, Nels Hoff. That October, upon complaint of several of the local residents, Cook and Hoff's liquor license was revoked when the Inyo County Board of Supervisors found "that said Hattie Cook…is a woman, that she tends bar, shakes dice, drinks liquors and becomes intoxicated in said premises; that said Hattie Cook is not a fit, proper or suitable person to be engaged in the selling of intoxicating liquor in Inyo County, California."

Further, it was discovered that Hattie Cook was better known by the alias Agnes Patrie, "a fat lady with shady reputation," according to the *Owens Valley Herald*. Cook/Patrie had "formerly conducted a house of ill fame in that region" and was probably the Mother Agnes who set up shop alongside Diamond Tooth Lil in Greenwater.

Later that month, in an unexpected turnabout, Nels Hoff circulated a petition in Death Valley Junction, signed by fifty-five people "who live or work at or near said town," including several Borax Company officials, asking that the board prohibit the sale of liquor entirely at the Junction. But the supervisors saw little point in dealing with the petition, as the county was about to go dry all over.

In 1911, under pressure from citizens in several districts, the county held district elections to determine how the residents felt about going dry. Of the five districts in Inyo County, only the fifth, which included most of Death Valley, voted to keep liquor legal. High times were to be had then in the Junction. By the end of 1914, the company had moved its ore roasting plant, and therefore a large number of its workers, to the Junction, and the prosperity of Tubb and others doing business on the west side of the tracks was assured.

The new regulations required that any applicant for a liquor license be vouched for by his neighbors. Tubb's status as "a sober and suitable person to carry on and conduct the business of selling intoxicating liquor" was guaranteed by his old friend R.J. "Dad" Fairbanks (the husband of Kitty's friend Celesta). Fairbanks was known as a hard drinker but was also widely respected as a desert pioneer.

By 1912, Kitty had come to realize that life as the matriarch of a "disreputable road house" clan didn't suit her. She and Bob separated

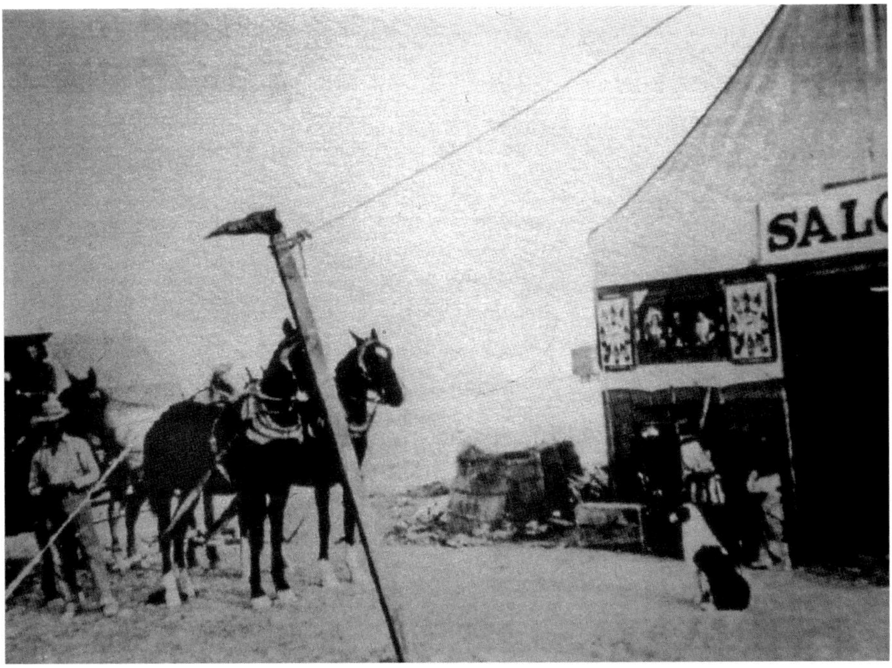

Tubb Saloon in Death Valley Junction, circa 1908. *Courtesy of Nancy Tubb Peterson, Judy Tubb and Virginia Tubb Goodsen.*

that year and divorced in 1914. Kitty moved with Danny across the state line into Ash Meadows, where she and Bob each then owned separate pieces of property. Kitty became a rancher and sometimes worked as a hotel cook. Today, her granddaughters still enjoy recounting family legends about Kitty's fine marksmanship and how she could shoot game for dinner from the front porch without ever getting out of her chair.

In her absence, business continued as usual at Tubb's establishment, though perhaps rather less organized. Frank Grace, who lived in Death Valley Junction in 1916, later recalled, "There were three girls named Bess in the village; one was a school teacher, another was an Indian, and the other a prostitute." The third Bess lived across the tracks, where the Amargosa Opera House is today, with another prostitute named Happy Days in a tin shack.

The end of 1916 saw countywide prohibition again in force, this time accompanied by a ban on gambling and with no out clause for the fifth district. By the end of November of that year, all establishments selling liquor were to cease and desist from such activity, and the exorbitant deposits given by Tubb and others for their licenses were returned. But an item in the *Inyo Register* in December 1916 claimed that Tubb had "suffered no curtailment of his privileges, though some report that the county had gone dry had reached camp."

Sources indicate that Tubb continued to maintain a brothel at the back of his store and saloon, but this probably didn't last long after the passage of the California Red Light Abatement Act in 1916. For over ten years, Tubb, in his isolated desert kingdom, had ignored a variety of laws, ordinances and attempts by the Borax Company to curtail his activities, but like it or not, the Progressive era was upon the nation, and civilization was settling in to Death Valley Junction.

Bob Tubb would eventually clean up his act and, through an extraordinary turn of events resulting from losses in a poker game, go into partnership in the hotel business with a respectable widow named Abbie Pierce. However, he also continued to operate a saloon and store at the Junction until he sold his property to the Borax Company in 1923.

"The so-called hotel was recently bought by us for purposes of getting rid of a saloon which attracted men with bootlegging liquor and for gambling," wrote a relieved company official to a higher-up. The Junction then became a family town.

Bob Tubb moved to Ash Meadows, and with him went the last of the wide-open Death Valley boom camps, red-light districts and tent saloons.

However, prostitution apparently continued to flourish on a small scale along the T&T Railroad tracks, especially at the stops of Silver Lake and Baker, until the rails were taken up for scrap during World War II. During the dismantling process in 1942, this item was reported to railroad officials from the small siding at Evelyn, between Death Valley Junction and Shoshone:

> *At about 5:30 pm yesterday, three colored whore ladies arrived at Evelyn, and quartered themselves in Section Foreman's house. At some time during the night, said to be midnight, a Mexican gentleman is said to have attacked a colored gentleman with a knife. The latter countered with a club, over former's head, breaking skull. Mexican friends took injured party to Death Valley Junction, and reported matter to Officer Brown.*

Mr. Brown was here at breakfast time to get evidence, and made arrests. 'Trial' is to be held at D.V.J. this day, 4:00 PM.

The whore ladies departed in their big Packard car, immediately after midnight melee.

And with those whore ladies went the end of an era.

BIBLIOGRAPHY

Chapters 1 and 2

Periodicals

Bakersfield Californian, November 13, 1912.

Coso Mining News, May 5, 1877; September 15, 1877.

Havilah Courier, March 6, 1868.

Inyo Independent, January 2, 1871; January 27, 1872; February 3, 1872; February 10, 1872; June 1, 1872; August 3, 1872; September 14, 1872; October 19, 1872; October 26, 1872; November 9, 1872; December 14, 1872; December 21, 1872; December 28, 1872; January 25, 1873; February 15, 1873; February 22, 1873; March 1, 1873; August 16, 1873; November 8, 1873; May 9, 1874; January 8, 1876; January 29, 1876; May 5, 1877; July 7, 1877; March 20, 1880; June 19, 1880; August 7, 1880; August 21, 1880; April 9, 1881; April 21, 1905.

Kern County Californian, March 31, 1883.

Los Angeles Herald, October 8, 1889.

Sacramento Daily Union, December 6, 1869; April 12, 1872.

Virginia City Territorial Enterprise, December 31, 1874.

BIBLIOGRAPHY

Primary Source Documents

Author's correspondence with John Gilmore, 2004.

Author's correspondence with Mike Patterson, owner of Cerro Gordo, 2004, interview 2005.

Bakersfield City Directory, 1911, 1912, 1913, 1915, 1917.

Baptismal Records Held at St. Malachy's Church, vol. 2 (1887–93) and vol. 3 (1893–1907). Tehachapi, Kern County.

Delinquent tax assessment rolls for Inyo County as published in *Inyo Independent*, 1874, 1875, 1876, 1880.

Inyo County Indices to "Delinquent Tax Collected," 1881–88 (Eastern California Museum).

Inyo County Marriage Records: Volume A, page 74 (Inyo County Recorder's Office).

Inyo County Mining Claims (Inyo County Recorder's Office).

Inyo County Property Records: Deeds, Books A–P (Inyo County Recorder's Office).

Inyo County "Property Taxes Paid" Register, 1874–80 (Eastern California Museum).

Inyo County Tax Assessment Rolls, 1881–86 (Eastern California Museum).

Kern County Death Records: Death Certificate Lola Cronin (Kern County Hall of Records).

Kern County Mining Claims (Kern County Hall of Records).

Kern County Probate Records: Distribution Decree (Kern County Hall of Records).

Kern County Property Records: Deeds (Kern County Hall of Records).

Ledger #1, Ledger #2, Meysan General Store, 1865–90 (Eastern California Museum).

"Log of Stage Coach Which Operated between Cerro Gordo Mine and Aurora, Nevada 1877–1878." Transcript in Eastern California Museum, Cerro Gordo information file.

Minutes, Inyo County Board of Supervisors, 1869–72 (Inyo County Recorder's Office).

Personal communication with Lola Gillespie Miller and Paul Gillespie, great-grandchildren of Lola Travis. September, October and December 2004.

Record of Attendance, Lone Pine School, 1883 (Eastern California Museum).

Record of Trader's License, Inyo County 1878–87 (Eastern California Museum).

U.S. Census, Alameda County, Murray Township, California, 1880.

———, Cerro Gordo, California, 1870.

———, Havilah, California, 1870.
———, Kern County, Township 2, California, 1900, 1910.
———, Lone Pine, California, 1870, 1880.
———, Stockton, California, 1920, 1930.
———, Tuolumne County, Township 1, California, 1850.
———, Ukiah, California, 1860.
———, Yavapai, Arizona Territory, 1900, 1910.

Books, Papers and Journal and Newspaper Articles

Boyd, William Harland. "Sageland: Its Rise and Fall." *Historic Kern, Kern County Historical Society Quarterly* (March 1969).

California Department of Parks and Recreation, Office of Historic Preservation. *Five Views: An Ethnic Historic Site Survey for California*. N.p., 1988.

Carrigan, William. "The Lynching of Persons of Mexican Origin or Descent in the United States, 1848 to 1928." *Journal of Social History* 37, no. 2 (2003).

Chalfant, W.A. *The Story of Inyo*. Bishop, CA: W.A. Chalfant, 1933.

Cragen, Dorothy Clora. *The Boys in the Sky Blue Pants: The Men and Events at Camp Independence and Forts of Eastern California, Nevada and Utah, 1862–1877*. Independence, CA, 1975.

Engle, Mike. "The Sageland Saga." *Desert Magazine*, December 1970.

Gonzalez, Deena J. *Refusing the Favor: The Spanish-Mexican Women of Santa Fe, 1820–1880*. New York: Oxford, 1999.

Gorman, Mrs. J.S. "The Story of Cerro Gordo: Romantic History of Inyo County Boom Town." *Inyo Independent*. Three-part series, undated. From Eastern California Museum Cerro Gordo information file.

Likes, Robert C. *Cerro Gordo Looking Back*. N.p.: Rosedog Press, 2010.

Likes, Robert C., and Glenn R. Day. *From This Mountain: Cerro Gordo*. Bishop, CA: Chalfant Press, 1975.

McClelland, Dr. Hugh K. "An Early Cerro Gordoan." *Inyo Register*. Original date unknown, reprint November 29, 1932.

———. "A Night in Cerro Gordo, 1872." *Inyo Register*. Original date unknown, reprint May 4, 1928.

Memorial and Biographical History of the Counties of Fresno, Tulare and Kern, California. Chicago: Lewis Publishing Company, 1892.

Nadeau, Remi. *The City Makers: The Story of Southern California's First Boom, 1868–1876*. N.p.: Interurban Press, 1977.

———. *Ghost Towns and Mining Camps of California*. Los Angeles: Ward Ritchie Press, 1965.

———. *The Silver Seekers: They Tamed California's Last Frontier*. Santa Barbara, CA: Crest Publishers, 1999.

Pitti, Jose, et al. "A History of Mexicans in America." *La Prensa San Diego*. N.p., n.d.

Purcell, Fernando. "Too Many Foreigners for My Taste: Law, Race and Ethnicity." In *Issues in Power and Violence*. N.p., n.d.

Sweetser, John. "Mojave Timeline." *Southern Pacific Trainline* (Winter 2002).

Taylor, Bayard. *Eldorado*. Vol. 1. 1850. Reprint, Alexandria, VA: Time Life Books, 1983.

Vargo, Cecile P. *Cerro Gordo*. Charleston, SC: Arcadia Publishing, 2012.

———. *Cerro Gordo: A Ghost Town Caught Between Centuries*. N.p.: Historical Society of the Upper Mojave Desert, 2012.

Chapter 3

Periodicals

Black Hills Daily Times, December 30, 1879; March 21, 1883; August 10, 1883; July 26, 1886.

California Police Gazette, May 2, 1868.

Chicago Republican, May 31, 1868.

Coso Mining News, April 22, 1876.

Inyo Independent, April 3, 1875; April 24, 1875.

Oakland Tribune, September 22, 1887; May 14, 1888; June 11, 1888; June 16, 1888; November 30, 1888.

Panamint News, February 23, 1875; March 2, 1875; March 13, 1875; March 18, 1875; March 23, 1875; March 27, 1875; November 6, 1875.

San Francisco Chronicle, June 16, 1885; October 1, 1885.

Virginia City Daily Trespass, May 3, 1867; May 13, 1867; May 14, 1867; May 24, 1867; June 27, 1867; October 8, 1867.

Virginia City Daily Union, January 21, 1867.

Virginia City Territorial Enterprise, January 22, 1867; February 3, 1867; June 27, 1867; October 3, 1874; November 19, 1874; November 25, 1874; November 28, 1874; December 23, 1874.

BIBLIOGRAPHY

Primary Source Documents

Divorce records 1871, 1872, Mercedes Nevarro (Nevada State Library and Archives microfilms).

H.B. Camp v. California Mining Company (microfilm, University of Nevada, Reno).

Herman B. Camp, biographical file in Douglas collection (Nevada State Historical Society, Reno).

Inyo County delinquent tax tolls, 1875, 1876 (Eastern California Museum).

Inyo County Marriage Records, vol. A (Inyo County Recorder's Office).

Inyo County Property Records: Deeds, Book F (Inyo County Recorder's Office).

Nevada State Census, 1875.

Second Directory of Nevada Territory, 1863.

State of Nevada v. John Millian (Nevada State Library and Archives).

Storey County Directory, 1871–72.

Storey County Marriages, Book A (Storey County Recorder's Office).

Storey County Mining Claims, Book A (microfilm).

St. Paul's Episcopal Church, Marriages, vol. 1, Virginia City (Nevada State Historical Society, Reno).

U.S. Census, Deadwood, Dakota Territory, 1880.

———, Virginia City, 1870, 1880.

Virginia City Directory, 1868–69.

Books, Papers and Journal and Newspaper Articles

Ayres, Ruth. "Newspaper Man in Panamint." *Lone Pine Progress-Citizen*, April 22, 1949.

Blackburn, George M., and Sherman L. Ricards. "The Prostitutes and Gamblers of Virginia City, Nevada: 1870." *Pacific Historical Review* (1979).

Clark, Walter Van Tilburg, ed. *The Journals of Alred Doten 1849–1903*. Reno: University of Nevada Press, 1975.

Daniels, Zeke. *The Life and Death of Julia C. Bulette, Queen of the Red Lights, Virginia City, Nevada*. Salinas, CA: El Camino Press, 1958.

DeLong, Charles. *The Life and Confessions of John Millian (Properly Jean Marie A. Villain) Convicted as the Murderer of Julia Bulette, as Given by Him to His Attorney.* Virginia City, NV: Lammon, Gregory & Palmer, 1868.

DeQuille, Dan. *The Big Bonanza*. New York: Alfred A. Knopf, 1953.

Diner, Hasia R. *Erin's Daughters in America: Irish Immigrant Women in the Nineteenth Century*. Baltimore, MD: Johns Hopkins University Press, 1983.

BIBLIOGRAPHY

Emrich, Duncan. *In the Delta Saloon: Conversations with Residents of Virginia City, Nevada.* Reno: University of Nevada Oral History Program, 1949–50.

Goldman, Marion. *Gold Diggers and Silver Miners: Prostitution and Social Life on the Comstock Lode.* Ann Arbor: University of Michigan Press, 1981.

———. "Prostitution and Virtue in Nevada." *Society* (1973).

Hegne, Barbara. *Harlots, Hurdies and Spirited Women of Virginia City, Nevada.* Medford, OR: FreeStyle Graphics, 2001.

James, Ronald M., and Elizabeth Raymond. *Comstock Women: The Making of a Mining Community.* Reno: University of Nevada Press, 1998.

Kimball, Nell. *Nell Kimball: Her Life as an American Madam.* New York: Macmillan Company, 1970.

Kinnersley, Thomas Harold. "Virginia, Nevada, 1859–1890: A Study of Police, Water, and Fire Problems." Unpublished dissertation, University of California–Los Angeles, 1974.

Leuba, Edmond. "A Frenchman in the Panamints." *California Historical Society Quarterly* 17, no. 3 (1938): 208–18.

Lingenfelter, Richard A. *Death Valley and the Amargosa: A Land of Illusion.* Berkeley: University of California Press, n.d.

Lord, Elliott. *Comstock Mining and Miners.* 1883. Reprint, Berkeley: Howell North, 1959.

Lyman, George D. *The Saga of the Comstock Lode: Boom Days in Virginia City.* New York: Charles Scribner's Sons, 1934.

MacKell, Jan. *Brothels, Bordellos and Bad Girls: Prostitution in Colorado 1860–1930.* Albuquerque: University of New Mexico Press, 2004.

McDonald, Douglas. *The Legend of Julia Bulette and the Red Light Ladies of Nevada.* Las Vegas: Nevada Publications, 1980.

McGrath, Robert T. *Gunfighters, Highwaymen and Vigilantes: Violence on the Frontier.* Berkeley: University of California Press, 1984.

Palazzo, Robert P. "The Death Valley Roots of Tombstone's Lawmen." *Proceedings, Fifth Death Valley Conference on History and Prehistory* (1999).

Rocha, Guy L. "Red Light Legend and Lore: Julia Bulette." Nevada State Archives Historical Myth a Month #20 and #122. 1997. dmla.clan.lib.nv.us/docs/nsla/archives/myth/myth20.htm.

Simmons, Alexy. "Red Light Ladies: Settlement Patterns and Material Culture on the Mining Frontier." *Anthropology Northwest* 4 (1989).

Traywick, Ben T. *Hell's Belles of Tombstone.* Tombstone, AZ: Red Marie's Book Store, 1993.

U.S. Marshal Service Website, History of the U.S. Marshals. "In the Matter of David Neagle." www.usmarshals.gov/history/neagle.htm.

Williams, George, III. *Rosa May: The Search for a Mining Camp Legend.* Dayton, NV: Tree by the River Publishing, 1984.
Wilson, Neill C. *Silver Stampede.* New York: MacMillan Company, 1937.

Chapter 4

Periodicals

Coso Mining News, May 19, 1877; August 4, 1877; September 15, 1877.
Inyo Independent, September 15, 1877; September 22, 1877; May 25, 1878; February 14, 1880; February 21, 1880.
Lusk Herald, May 14, 1964; March 24, 1999.
Marysville Daily Appeal, November 3, 1866.
Montana Post, April 20, 1867.
Rocky Mountain News, June 18, 1863; May 17, 1864.

Primary Source Documents

Inyo County delinquent tax rolls, 1875, as published in the *Inyo Independent.*
Inyo County Indices to Delinquent Tax Collected 1881–88 (Eastern California Museum).
Inyo County Indices to Property Tax Collected 1874–80 (Eastern California Museum).
Inyo County Minutes of Probate Court, vol. A (records stored by the Eastern California Museum at the Inyo County Courthouse).
Inyo County Probate Order and Decrees, vol. A (records stored by the Eastern California Museum at the Inyo County Courthouse).
Inyo County Property Records: Deeds, Book G (Inyo County Recorder's Office).

Books, Papers and Journal and Newspaper Articles

Bancroft, Hubert Howe. "The Works of Hubert Howe Bancroft, vol. 36." *Popular Tribunals* 1, no. 35 (n.d.)
Cragen, Dorothy Clora. Untitled manuscript regarding the killing of Nancy Williams. In the Darwin information file at the Eastern California Museum.

Lingenfelter, Richard. *Death Valley & the Amargosa: Land of Illusion*. Berkeley: University of California Press, 1986.
Palazzo, Robert P. *Darwin, California*. Lake Grove, OR: Western Places, 1996.
Roberts, Oliver de la Fontaine. "The Death Valley Kid." *Pony Express Courier*, August 1953; November 1954; January 1955; March 1957
———. *The Great Understander.* N.p.: William Walker Press, 1932.
Rottenberg, Dan. *Death of a Gunfighter: The Quest for Jack Slade, the West's Most Elusive Legend*. N.p.: Westholme Publishing, 2010.
Thorp, Russell. "Old Mother Featherlegs Shepard." Typewritten manuscript in the collection of the Stagecoach Museum, Lusk, Wyoming.
Webb, Rena. "Girls of the Gulch: Ol' Mother Featherlegs." *Deadwood Magazine*, March/April 1997.

Chapter 5

Periodicals

Coso Mining News, November 13, 1875; March 20, 1875; April 29, 1876.
Inyo Independent, June 1, 1872.
Panamint News, March 20, 1875.
Territorial Enterprise, June 22, 1867.

Primary Source Documents

Inyo County Marriage Records, vol. A (Inyo County Recorder's Office).
"Log of Stagecoach Which Operated between Cerro Gordo Mine and Aurora, Nevada 1877–1878." Transcript in Eastern California Museum Cerro Gordo information file.
U.S. Census, Darwin, CA, 1880.

Books, Papers and Journal and Newspaper Articles

Asbury, Herbert. *The Barbary Coast: An Informal History of the San Francisco Underworld*. Reprint, n.p.: Thunder's Mouth Press, 2002.

Butler, Anne M. *Daughters of Joy, Sisters of Misery: Prostitutes in the American West 1865–90*. Urbana: University of Illinois Press, 1985.

Edwards, Sue. "Chinese Prostitution on the Comstock Lode: 1860–1880." Master's thesis, University of Nevada–Reno, 1983.

Evans, Albert S. *A la California: Sketch of Life in the Golden State*. San Francisco: A.L. Bancroft & Company, 1873.

Goldman, Marion. *Gold Diggers and Silver Miners: Prostitution and Social Life on the Comstock Lode*. Ann Arbor: University of Michigan Press, 1981.

James, Ronald. *The Roar and the Silence: A History of Virginia City and the Comstock Lode*. Reno: University of Nevada Press, 1998.

Palazzo, Robert. *Darwin, California*. Lake Grove, OR: Western Places, 1996.

Sandmeyer, Elmer Clarence. *The Anti-Chinese Movement in California*. Urbana: University of Illinois Press, 1973.

Seagraves, Anne. *Soiled Doves: Prostitution in the Early West*. Hayden, ID: Wesanne Publications, 1994.

Tong, Benson. *Unsubmissive Women: Chinese Prostitution in Nineteenth-Century San Francisco*. Norman: University of Oklahoma Press, 1994.

Chapters 6 and 7

Periodicals

Anaconda Standard, December 1, 1900; December 16, 1900; December 18, 1900; December 19, 1900; March 10, 1901; March 12, 1901; March 13, 1901; March 15, 1901; April 7, 1901; August 4, 1901; August 24, 1901; December 16, 1901; April 9, 1903; August 10, 1903; August 13, 1903; September 14, 1903; September 17, 1903; January 1, 1904; June 16, 1904; June 17, 1904; June 19, 1904; June 22, 1904; November 6, 1909.

Ballard News, January 17, 1908.

Beatty Bullfrog Miner, January 4, 1907; June 22, 1907; July 13, 1907; August 10, 1907; August 31, 1907; October 5, 1907; November 2, 1907; November 9, 1907; November 14, 1907; December 21, 1907; January 4, 1908; January 11, 1908; January 18, 1908; February 8, 1908; March 29, 1908; April 18, 1908; August 15, 1908.

Manhattan Mail, October 30, 1909.

Nevada State Journal, June 2, 1936; June 4, 1936; December 3, 1937; December 25, 1938; July 19, 1961; July 23, 1961.

Rawhide Rustler, May 2, 1908; May 8, 1908.

Reno Evening Gazette, October 15, 1912; September 16, 1915; November 6, 1923; December 15, 1937; July 15, 1938.

Rhyolite Daily Bulletin, January 4, 1908; January 7, 1908; January 8, 1908; January 11, 1908; January 13, 1908; January 17, 1908; January 21, 1908; February 5, 1908; February 20, 1908; February 26, 1908; March 26, 1908; March 27, 1908; March 28, 1908; March 30, 1908; April 1, 1908.

Rhyolite Herald, January 18, 1907; November 22, 1907; May 5, 1908; August 19, 1908.

Tonopah Daily Bonanza, January 4, 1908; January 5, 1908; January 7, 1908; January 8, 1908; January 9, 1908; February 18, 1908; March 24, 1908; March 25, 1908; March 26, 1908; March 27, 1908; March 28, 1908; March 29, 1908; April 2, 1908; September 30, 1912; October 1, 1912; October 2, 1912; October 4, 1912; October 10, 1912; October 12, 1912; October 14, 1912; October 16, 1912; September 20, 1913; November 16, 1923.

Tonopah Daily Sun, November 6, 1907; November 11, 1907; November 22, 1907; November 23, 1907; January 16, 1908; March 23, 1908; April 1, 1908.

Primary Source Documents

California Death Index.

Dawes County, Chadron, Nebraska. Marriage certificate for S. Isabel Peterman and Clinton C. Heskett, April 14, 1906 (Dawes County Historical Society).

Defendant's Exhibit A, State of Nevada v. Skinner: Map of dwelling house on Lot 18, Block 16, Townsite of Rhyolite, Nevada. Filed March 24, 1908 (Central Nevada Museum).

Emery and Carrie Peterman Family Tree (compiled by Francis Xavier Barden).

Grand County, Colorado, Court Records.

Nevada State Penitentiary at Carson City, Prisoner Record for Fred Skinner covering 1908 through 1940 (Nevada State Library and Archives).

Nye County Court Minutes, vol. C (Nye County Clerk's Office).

Nye County Death Records, vol. A, A.G. Cable (Nye County Recorder's Office).

Personal correspondence with Francis Xavier Barden, descendant of the Peterman family.

Property tax assessment rolls for the city of Rhyolite, 1908–15 (Nye County Recorder's Office).

Skinner v. Skinner, 1911, Divorce Decree granted (Washoe County Clerk's Office).

State v. F.E. Davis, I.C. Levy and Mona Bell, 1907 (Nye County Clerk's Office).

State v. Skinner, Case #1908, Nevada Supreme Court Case Files (UNLV Law Library).

U.S. Census, Barton, Vermont, 1860, 1870, 1880, 1910.

———, Carson City, Nevada, 1910, 1920.

———, Coshocton, Ohio, 1870.

———, Lead, South Dakota, 1900.

———, Los Angeles, California, 1910, 1920.

———, Reno, Nevada, 1930.

———, Rhyolite, Nevada, 1910.

———, Seattle, Washington, 1910, 1920.

———, Smithfield, Iowa, 1870.

Washington State Death Index.

Books, Papers and Journal and Newspaper Articles

Anderson, J.J. Unpublished letter to Ruth Woodman/Death Valley Days, 1934. Ruth Woodman papers, University of Oregon Knight Special Collections Library.

Brown, Dora Eugene Boyd. Unpublished reminiscences of life in Rhyolite on file at the Death Valley National Park Archives.

Carruthers, William. 1951. *Loafing Along Death Valley Trails*. Ontario, CA: Death Valley Publishing Company, n.d.

Coughlin, Kari. Survivors Reunion transcript, 1993. On file at the Death Valley National Park Archives.

———. Survivors Reunion transcript, 1995. On file at the Death Valley National Park Archives.

Flinchum, Robin. "Rhyolite, Nevada." Nevada Online Encyclopedia Project. University of Nevada Humanities Committee. 2005.

Latschar, John A. *Historic Resource Study: A History of Mining in Death Valley*. Denver, CO: U.S. Department of the Interior, National Park Service, 1981.

McCoy, Suzy. *Rebecca's Walk Through Time*. N.p.: self-published, 2005.

Metscher, Allen. "Beating of Laura "Tex" Watson at the Monte Carlo, Rhyolite, Nevada." Unpublished notes from Allen Metscher's personal collection.

Murgarber, Nell. "Ghost Town Dwellers." *Desert Magazine*, February 1959.

Patera, Alan. *Rhyolite: The Boom Years.* Lake Grove, OR: Western Places, 1994.
———. *Rhyolite's Demise.* Lake Grove, OR: Western Places, 2004.
Presser, E. Louise. "Memoirs of E. Louise Presser, Rhyolite, 1906–1908." *Nevada Historical Society Quarterly* (Summer 1972).
Ritter, Betsy. *Life in the Ghost City of Rhyolite.* Terra Bella, CA: Terra Bella News, 1982.
Stetz, Deborah Anne. "Life in the Last Boomtown: Rhyolite, Nevada, 1905–1912." Master's thesis, University of San Diego, 1993.
———. Survivors Reunion transcript, 1992. On file at the Death Valley National Park Archives.
Weight, Harold, and Lucille Weight. *Rhyolite: Death Valley's Ghost City of Golden Dreams.* Reprint, Death Valley, CA: Death Valley Natural History Association, 1996.

Chapter 8

Periodicals

Cleveland Plain Dealer, April 22, 1900.
Elyria, Ohio, Chronicle Telegram, January 19, 1939.
Goldfield Chronicle, January 7, 1909.
Idaho Daily Statesman, January 19, 1945; November 7, 1963; September 8, 1967.
Idaho Statesman, August 15, 1914; October 12, 1922; July 18, 1926; September 29, 1970.
Las Vegas Review Journal, October 5, 1944; January 3, 1949.
Pomona Progress Bulletin, September 7, 1967; September 8, 1967.
Reno Evening Gazette, December 18, 1902.
San Bernardino Sun Telegram, January 24, 1960.
Sandusky Register, March 20, 1895.
Youngstown Daily Vindicator, March 16, 1895; March 18, 1895; March 19, 1895; March 20, 1895.
Youngstown Vindicator, October 23, 1934.

BIBLIOGRAPHY

Primary Source Documents

Author's personal communication with Anita Lewis regarding her mother's friendship with Lil, August 2003.

Author's personal communication with Carrie Schikora, great-granddaughter of Evelyn Hildegard, 2014, 2015.

Author's personal communication with Helen Echevarria regarding her acquaintance with Lil while Lil was running a bar in Boise, Idaho, November 2003.

Author's personal communication with Mildred Myers, RN, regarding her care of Lil during Lil's last days in a Pomona nursing home, November 2003.

Author's personal communication with Ruth Osborne, RN, regarding her care of Lil during Lil's last days in a Pomona nursing home, November 2003.

Author's personal communication with Vance Gilliam, descendant of the Fairbanks family, regarding relationship and communication between Celesta Fairbanks and Diamond Tooth Lil, July 2003.

Boise, Idaho, city directories, 1921–43.

Coroner's Report of Inquisition on the body of Michael Fialla, March 20, 1895, Mahoning County Coroner's Office.

Court documents relating to arrest of Evelyn Hildegard, September 10, 1925, charged with keeping a disorderly house, Mahoning County Courthouse.

Death certificate of Evelyn Hildegard, Pomona, California, September 3, 1967.

Death certificate of John J. Fialla, Pomona California, March 15, 1961.

Death Index, Ward 3, Youngstown, Mahoning County, Ohio.

Death Valley Days scripts (various) in U.S. Borax Company archives.

Declaration of Intention (to become U.S. citizen), Michael Fialla, June 4, 1909, Mahoning County, Ohio.

Decree of Annulment, Evelyn Houck/Carl Houck, Boise, 1920, Mahoning County Vital Records Office.

Goldfield, Nevada, city directory, 1907–08.

Letter from Evelyn Hildegard to Mrs. Tucker, 1954, from Idaho Historical Society collection.

Marriage License #3578, R.L. Miller/E. Hildegard, Mount Vernon, Washington, 1912.

Marriage License #7106, Evelyn Hildegard/Albert Gambil, Boise, Idaho, 1925.

Marriage License #42050, Evelyn Hildegard/Andrew Marker, Mountain Home, Idaho, 1928.

Marriage License #106195, Evelyn Hildegard/Carl Houk, Emmett, Idaho, 1920.

BIBLIOGRAPHY

Notes and photographs sent by Evelyn Hildegard to her daughter, in possession of Carrie Schikora.

Papers and letters in the Fred Mazzulla collection of the Colorado Historical Society.

Petition for Divorce and Restraining Order, *Minnie B. Davis v. Jack Davis*, December 23, 1908, Esmeralda County, Nevada.

Register of Criminal Actions, Ada County, Idaho, *State of Idaho v. Evelyn Hildegar*, September 12, 1925.

Sanborn Insurance Map of Youngstown, Ohio, 1900.

San Diego City Directory, 1918.

Unpublished notes from the research materials of Ruth Woodman (who wrote all the radio and television scripts for the program *Death Valley Days* between 1930 and 1945) in the Special Collections Department of the University of Oregon.

Unpublished photograph in the possession of Vance Gilliam connecting Death Valley's Diamond Tooth Lil to Evelyn Hildegard.

U.S. Census, Boise, Idaho, 1930, 1940.

———, El Centro, California, 1920.

———, Lake View, Oregon, 1910.

———, Youngstown, Ohio, 1900, 1910, 1920.

Youngstown, Ohio, city directories, 1899–1923.

Books, Papers and Journal and Newspaper Articles

Alexander, Anabelle. *Oral History of Thomas Berry*. Boise: Idaho Oral History Center, Idaho State Historical Society, 1969.

———. *Oral History of Viola B. Tucker*. Boise: Idaho Bicentennial Commission's and Idaho Historical Society's Oral History Project, 1975.

American Historical Society. *History of Ohio*. Vol. 4, *Biography of Michael Fialla*. N.p., 1925.

Barnhart, Jacqueline Baker. *The Fair but Frail: Prostitution in San Francisco, 1849–1900*. Reno: University of Nevada Press, 1986.

Belden, L. Burr. *Mines of Death Valley*. N.p.: La Siesta Press, 1966.

Cantwell, Robert. *The Real McCoy: The Life and Times of Norman Selby*. Princeton, NJ: Auerbach Publishers Inc., 1971.

Carruthers, William. *Loafing Along Death Valley Trails*. Ontario, CA: Death Valley Publishing Company, 1951.

BIBLIOGRAPHY

Clawson, Elliott J. "The Sheriff of Greenwater: A Story of the Death Valley Slope." Parts I and II. *Overland Monthly* (1909).

"'Diamondfield' Jack Davis: One of the Richest and Most Generous Hearted of Nevada's Miners—His Romantic Life." From "Portraits and Biographies of Prominent Engineers, Miners and Businessmen of Nevada." *Successful American* (August 1906).

Doughty, Nan. "Bullfrog-Rhyolite and Jim Moffat's Prophecy." *Central Nevada's Glorious Past* 3, no. 1 (May 1980).

Drago, Harry Sinclair. *Notorious Ladies of the Frontier*. New York: Dodd, Mead & Company, 1969.

Glass, Mary Ellen. *The Life of a Newsboy in Nevada: An Oral History of Joseph McDonald*. Reno: University of Nevada Oral History Project, 1971.

Glasscock, C.B. *Gold in Them Hills*. New York: Grosset and Dunlap, 1932.

———. *Here's Death Valley.* New York: Grosset and Dunlap, 1940.

Grover, David. *Diamondfield Jack: A Study in Frontier Justice*. Reno: University of Nevada Press, 1968.

Hamilton, Marybeth. *When I'm Bad, I'm Better: Mae West, Sex, and American Entertainment.* New York: HarperCollins Publishers, 1995.

Hanna, Phil, et al. *Death Valley Tales.* Death Valley '49ers Encampment Keepsake. Bishop, CA: Chalfant Press, 1955.

Harvey, Karen. *Daring Daughters: Saint Augustine's Feisty Females, 1565–2000.* Virginia Beach, VA: Donning Company, 2002.

Hildegard, Evelyn, and Ruth Ellen Smith. "I Was Known as Diamond Tooth Lil." Undated clipping from an unidentified magazine, probably late 1940s (in the archives of the Idaho State Historical Society).

Holloway, Winona J. "Oral History of George Ishmael: Pioneer of Death Valley and the Amargosa." In *Proceedings, Fourth Death Valley Conference on History and Prehistory, February 2–5, 1995.*

Jones, Nard. *Seattle.* Garden City, NY: Doubleday & Company, Inc., 1972.

Kimball, Nell. *Nell Kimball: Her Life as an American Madam*. New York: Macmillan Company, 1970.

King, R.T. "Women, Children and Family Life in the Nevada Interior, 1900–1930s." In *Memories of Austin, Bodie and Goldfield, 1900–1910*. Edited by Lena Hammond. Reno: University of Nevada Oral History Program, 1987.

Maclane, John F. *A Sagebrush Lawyer*. New York: Pandick Press, 1953.

Martin, Cy. *Whiskey and Wild Women*. New York: Hart Publishing Company, 1970.

Moe, Al. *The Roots of Reno*. N.p.: BookSurge Publishing, 2008.

Morgan, Lael. *Good Time Girls of the Alaska-Yukon Gold Rush*. Kenmore, WA: Epicenter Press, 1998.
O'Brien, Dan. "How Youngstown's Other Half Lived." *Business Journal Online*, January 2000.
Russell, JoAnne. "A Necessary Evil: Prostitutes, Patriarchs and Profit in Boise City, 1863–1915." Master's thesis, Boise Sate University, 1991.
Sorrells, Susan. *Charlie & Stella Brown*. Death Valley '49ers Encampment Keepsake. Shoshone, CA: Death Valley Publishing Company, 1979.
Stohler, Betty J. *Death Valley Helen Tells This*. San Bernardino, CA: self-published, 1981.
Ward, Carol M. *Mae West: A Bio-Bibliography*. New York: Greenwood Press, 1989.
West, Mae. *Diamond Lil*. New York: Dell Publishing Company, Inc., 1932.
Whelehan, Patricia. *An Anthropological Perspective on Prostitution*. Lewiston, NY: Edwin Mellen Press, 2001.
Zanjani, Sally. *The Glory Days in Goldfield, Nevada*. Reno: University of Nevada Press, 2002.
———. *Goldfield: The Last Gold Rush on the Western Frontier*. Athens: Ohio University Press, 1992.

Chapter 9

Periodicals

Inyo Independent, June 4, 1909.
Inyo Register, September 5, 1907; February 18, 1909; November 3, 1910; December 14, 1916.
Owens Valley Herald, October 15, 1909.

Primary Source Documents

Interview with Virginia Goodsen and Judy Tubb, Beatty, Nevada, 2003.
Liquor license application, Bob Tubb.
Liquor license application, Martin Picco, 1913.
Petition to the Inyo County Board of Supervisors from residents of Death Valley Junction, 1909, from the Eastern California Museum collection.

T&T Daily Report from Evelyn, September 23, 1942 (from the T&T collection at the Huntington Archives).

Unpublished notes from the Ruth Woodman collection at the Knight Special Collections Library, University of Oregon.

U.S. Census, Ash Meadows, Nevada, 1920.

———, Death Valley Junction, California, 1910, 1920.

———, Tuscarora, Pennsylvania, 1870, 1880.

Books, Papers and Journal and Newspaper Articles

Glasscock, C.B. *Gold in Them Hills*. New York: Grosset and Dunlap, 1932.

———. *Here's Death Valley*. New York: Grosset and Dunlap, 1940.

Gower, Harry. *Fifty Years in Death Valley: Memoirs of a Borax Man*. San Bernardino, CA: Inland Printing, Inc., 1969.

Grace, Frank. "The First Death Valley Junction School Teacher." Unpublished reminiscence on file at the Shoshone Museum, circa 1975.

Lewis, Georgia. "Classic Desert Clash over Junction Virtue." *Nevada West and Pahrump Valley Times*, April 1975

———. "Death Valley Junction." *Nevadan*, June 25, 1972.

———. "Real Shotgun Kitty Bigger Than Life." *Pahrump Valley Times*, April 1973.

———. "Sad Times at Amargosa." *Nevadan*, January 16, 1972.

Travis, N.J., and E.J. Cocks. *The Tincal Trail: A History of Borax*. London: Harrap Limited, 1984.

Vincent, Bill. "Ash Meadows Yesterday and Today." *Nevadan*, December 28, 1969.

ABOUT THE AUTHOR

Over twenty years ago, on a hot day in the ghost town of Rhyolite, I looked through a dusty window and read a brief story about the murder of a prostitute named Mona Bell in the red-light district. It was only a few short lines on an old bit of paper, but I still remember it because it gave me a human connection to the rubble and debris that had once been a part of this disappeared city. I knew there were stories here; I could feel them, almost hear them whispering as I walked the abandoned streets. And I knew I would have to find them and tell them, one way or another.

I didn't live in the desert then, but it took only one visit to Death Valley to captivate me completely, and I returned as often as I could. Eventually, the time between visits began to feel like a dull limbo that must be endured until I could get back to where I knew I belonged. Finally, with next to nothing in my pocket and a rickety travel trailer to live in, I moved to Tecopa. Since then, I have worked as a freelance journalist covering the Death Valley region, had the honor of helping to organize the first ever Death Valley Women's History exhibit at the Shoshone Museum, got married and spent over twelve years writing the book that is now called *Red Light Women of Death Valley*. A good part of those years was given over not to writing but to reveling in the great good fortune of being a mother and now a homeschooling parent to my son. Along with my husband and son, I still live in Tecopa, where the view goes on forever, the sky is wide open and the history continues to speak to me.